CINEMA OF THE 70S

101 ICONIC MOVIES

DEDICATION

For my father, John “Skip” Foote,
My best friend, and the man who first introduced me to movies.
Those late nights on the couch watching Fright Night Theatre
Are foggy with time,
But the spark they lit burns bright.
Sitting close to you, to be safe,
Your arms around my brother and me,
The smell of your Old Spice,
As Chaney, Karloff and Lagosi worked their magic on that black-and-white TV,
In that dark living room so long ago.
In my life, I have known no better man than you, Dad.
This is for you.

JHF

First published in 2023 by Palazzo Editions Ltd
15 Church Road
London SW13 9HE
www.palazzoeditions.com

A CIP catalogue record for this book is available from the British Library.
ISBN 9781786751331

Bound and printed in China
10 9 8 7 6 5 4 3 2 1
Designed by Sarah Pyke for Palazzo Editions

CINEMA OF THE 70S

101 ICONIC MOVIES

PALAZZO

CONTENTS

INTRODUCTION

In 1964, folk singer Bob Dylan sang the anthem "The Times They Are a-Changin'", calling his generation to action. It was a time of turmoil and cultural revolution brought on by the assassinations of President John F. Kennedy, his brother Senator Robert, and Civil Rights Leader Martin Luther King. The subsequent conspiracy and cover-up of the presidential assassination brought about a staggering lack of trust in government. America had joined a war in Vietnam, a place many Americans would struggle to find on a map. Yet they were sending their young men to die there. Protests and marches erupted across the country. Music, theatre, literature, journalism, and film began to reflect changes on the political front.

Hollywood was slowly dying through the 60s, and everyone knew it. The big-budget studio films were no longer a draw for the audiences who were more sophisticated and informed than any generation before them. They did not want to see silly fantasies on the big screen; they wanted hard truths and life reflected in their movies. Thus, big-budget films like *The Alamo* (1960), *Mutiny on the Bounty* (1962), *Cleopatra* (1963), *Doctor Dolittle* (1967), *Star!* (1968), and *Hello, Dolly!* (1969) were massive failures at the box office and with critics. Smaller, more intimate films like *Psycho* (1960), *The Hustler* (1961), *To Kill a Mockingbird* (1962), *Hud* (1963), and *Dr. Strangelove* (1964) held greater interest for audiences than the studio fare.

The established directors were out of touch with their audiences and unwilling to evolve. Meanwhile, a new generation of film directors was studying in college, learning about the aesthetics and history of cinema, feeding a love of film that was unquenchable. Exciting new plays were opening on Broadway that would later become films, notably *Who's Afraid of Virginia Woolf?* (1966), which tackled societal conventions, sex, and the study of a dysfunctional marriage. Rave reviews greeted the film, along with solid box office returns and thirteen Academy Award nominations. Hollywood was beginning to understand. The world was changing, and movies needed to follow suit.

It came to a head in 1967, a watershed year in Hollywood, the beginning of the end for the studio system; the old formula replaced by hits such as *Bonnie and Clyde*, *The Graduate*, *In the Heat of the Night*, and *In Cold Blood*. Each spoke to the times in a way that resonated with modern audiences.

Employing techniques of the French New Wave, *Bonnie and Clyde* dealt with two famous bank robbers and killers of the Great Depression. "They're young...they're in love...and they kill people," screamed the ads for the film, which spoke to the youth of the 60s, reminding them that only a few decades earlier, young people had felt restless and disenfranchised as well.

Bonnie and Clyde became a sensation, nominated for ten Academy Awards, and a box office smash. Critics disparaged the film when it opened, but many wrote retractions after seeing it a second and third time, not being able to shake the movie from their minds. The film openly dealt with issues surrounding sexuality, including nymphomania and impotence; the characters were attractive but, ultimately, killers.

The Graduate spoke directly to the young people feeling that same aimlessness and boredom with their life after college. Young Benjamin Braddock (Dustin Hoffman) enters a purely sexual affair with his mother's best friend, the older Mrs. Robinson (Anne Bancroft). But then Benjamin complicates his life by falling in love with Mrs. Robinson's daughter. The film's final shot shows him and the daughter together at the back of a bus, but their smiles fade as they begin to think of what lies ahead, a "what now?" look crossing over them. The new style of film said so much with a single image, and that final image from *The Graduate* spoke volumes to so many.

Stanley Kubrick's astounding *2001: A Space Odyssey* (1968) dared audiences to go on a journey to challenge all their beliefs. Bear in mind, man had not yet landed on the moon, yet Kubrick gave audiences a vision of space that was realistic and beautiful at the same time. Taking us from prehistoric times, when ape-like men learn how to kill for food, land, and power, through to a man on Jupiter being reborn, the film swept audiences away in its narrative. Kubrick's film expanded cinema, using classical music, special effects, cinematography, and sound to reach new heights. And that treacherous computer, a sign of the future? Listening to the HAL 9000 die was haunting and poignant, yet we knew we were watching a killer die.

When *Midnight Cowboy* (1969) won the Academy Award for Best Picture, an X-rated film, the old Hollywood officially died. The New American cinema had been launched and would continue to evolve into the 70s and beyond. Exciting and

"The established directors were out of touch with their audiences and unwilling to evolve."

emerging directors began to explore previously taboo topics, no longer burdened by censorship of language, subject matter, or sexuality. More importantly, these new directors were bursting with ideas about how to merge the great films of the past they so loved with their fresh ideas.

Today, half a century later, great films are measured by those of the 70s. Has there been a more impactful decade? Not in my opinion. For the first time, cinema reflected life and society, presenting both on the big screen with a compelling and penetrating truth. Directors became household names, often overnight, and films routinely broke box office records.

With censorship relaxed, the subject matter could include alienation, descents into madness, drug addiction, dysfunctional relationships, promiscuity, alcoholism, PTSD, and any big news story of the day. Audiences gladly absorbed this new, shocking reality; in fact, they avoided films that candy-coated the truth.

Musicals evolved; westerns all but died for several years; science fiction and fantasy made an incredible resurgence; and horror dominated the box office along with disaster films. But by and large, films about social issues were the best draw.

This book celebrates the cinema of the 70s. What a decade!

JOHN H. FOOTE

14

FIVE EASY PIECES (1970)

DIRECTED BY Bob Rafelson
COUNTRY USA

Opposite Nicholson is equally believable as the trouble-making blue-collar worker as he is the privileged piano prodigy.

After his superb performance as George Hanson in *Easy Rider* (1969), which won him the New York Film Critics Award for Best Supporting Actor and an Academy Award nomination, Jack Nicholson was on the cusp of major stardom. *Five Easy Pieces* was the film that completed his path to being America's newest great actor and the embodiment of the 1970s anti-hero.

As Bobby Dupea, we first encounter him on an oil field where he works with his buddy, raises hell, and generally lives the blue-collar life. Yet there is something different about Bobby that sets him apart from the rest of his crowd. We soon learn that he was a piano prodigy from an affluential family and that he walked away from it all. When his father suffers a stroke, Bobby returns home to see the ailing man for the first time in many years. Despite his misgivings, he takes his annoying girlfriend Rayette (Karen Black) with him, knowing she will be the object of jokes and scorn among his elitist family.

Bobby quickly recalls why he left in the first place—the pretense and superiority of his siblings disgust him. He understands why they dislike Rayette because he can barely tolerate her, but he hates watching them humiliate her.

Ultimately, he abandons her at a gas station and hitches a ride north, knowing he will eventually hurt her, so she is better off without him. Bobby is a nomad who is better off on his own. But he is not without feelings. The scene where he breaks down while trying to communicate with his father is truly memorable. The sobs escape him with a fury. Though he does all the talking, he learns more about himself than he ever knew.

Nicholson is brilliant as Bobby, a revelation as a character actor. Loathing rules and authority of any kind, his famous scene in the restaurant where he tries to order a piece of toast remains one of the most iconic moments in American film. Audiences fell in love with Nicholson at that moment.

Both he and Karen Black were Oscar nominees for the film, which collected the New York Film Critics Award as Best Picture, but Nicholson finished runner-up to George C. Scott in *Patton* (1970). The film remains a landmark of the 70s and firmly established Rafelson as a filmmaker of note and Nicholson as a bankable talent. Very few movies from this era captured the restless spirit of youth as effectively as this did.

“Nicholson is brilliant as Bobby, a revelation as a character actor.”

16

"The actors are gritty and authentic, so real that they give the movie almost a documentary feel."

GOIN' DOWN THE ROAD (1970)

DIRECTED BY Donald Shebib
COUNTRY Canada

Goin' Down the Road exploded out of Canada in 1970, an unassuming little film shot on 16mm, using short ends, in and around Toronto. The budget was only $78,000 and expectations were low, but it turned into a cultural phenomenon, an extraordinary work that captured Toronto as it was in 1970, before the CN Tower joined the skyline. The scenes in Cape Breton were actually on Cherry Beach in Toronto and other areas adjacent to the city.

At the time, no one noticed Canadian cinema other than their documentaries or National Film Board animations or shorts. Here, finally, was a narrative film about life in Canada.

Two blue-collar men from Cape Breton—known as "Maritimers" or "Newfies"—come to the city seeking better jobs, better pay, and women. Pete (Doug McGrath) and Joey (Paul Bradley) load up Joey's boat of a car and head across Highway 401 to the big city. They love the Toronto nightlife but find getting work every bit as difficult as it was back home. They finally get hired at a bottling factory. Barely scraping by to their next pay cheque, Joey is content with his life, but Pete is not. He wants more and is restless. Joey meets a young woman who soon gets pregnant, and they get married. But then they are laid off from the bottling factory, and the three squeeze into a one-room apartment, near destitute.

Desperate, they steal a load of groceries from a local store. When a young clerk suspects them and follows them out of the store, they assault him and drive away. Knowing they are in trouble, they leave the city and head west for a new chance. There are no smiles on this trip: Joey has left behind his pregnant wife and a life he loved, and Pete, though he attempts a brave face, is equally distraught. The promise of a better life in Toronto never transpired, and they are again "goin' down the road."

Instant acclaim greeted the film when it began screening in Canada and the United States. A theatre in New York City screened it for a staggering six months, filling the theatre almost every night. In Canada, it was a first—a film by Canadians, for Canadians, and about Canadians. And best of all, it was universally embraced by Canadian audiences.

The actors are gritty and authentic, so real that they give the movie almost a documentary feel. Doug McGrath is superb, and Bradley, often the comic relief in the film, equally fine. Jayne Eastwood as Betty, the woman Joey marries, is also excellent. She went on to a successful career in Canadian film and television.

Shebib believed in Canada and wanted to help create a film culture back home. He had studied with no less than Francis Ford Coppola, with whom he shared big dreams for Canadian cinema. Sadly, it never took place. When I spoke with him thirty years after *Goin' Down the Road*, he had become a bitter and cynical man, as disappointed in himself as he was in the Canadian film industry. He would make a sequel entitled *Down the Road Again* (2011), which picks up the story forty years later with Pete, now living in British Columbia. He receives news that Joey has died and agrees to return his friend's ashes to Cape Breton. On the journey, he follows directions from Joey through a series of letters and at last finds a happy ending.

Goin' Down the Road came just one year after the Oscar-winning *Midnight Cowboy* (1969) and shares with the film that down and dirty realism of a city perceived to be gleaming with hope and providing nothing but despair. Each is, in its own right, a masterful piece of cinema.

Opposite This iconic Canadian film set the bar high for those that followed in the 70s. Few achieved it.

18 LOVE STORY (1970)

DIRECTED BY Arthur Hiller
COUNTRY USA

Opposite The chemistry between MacGraw and O'Neal won the hearts of audiences.

Although some passed over this film as sentimental tripe, the impact upon its release in 1970 was staggering. Audiences openly wept as they exited the theatre, overcome by the film's tragic ending. The soundtrack became among the most famous ever composed, and young Ryan O'Neal and Ali MacGraw became the new kids in Hollywood. The phrase "love means never having to say you're sorry" is still quoted today. The movie just seemed to come along at precisely the right time when everyone needed a good cry. Though there had been "tearjerkers" in theatres before, and many would follow, nothing seems to compare with *Love Story*.

Oliver Barrett IV (O'Neal) meets Jenny Cavilleri (MacGraw) at Harvard, where he attends school. His family is immensely wealthy, and she comes from a working-class family who have managed to save enough money to send her to college on a scholarship for music at nearby Radcliffe College. They fall in love, much to the chagrin of his family, who cut off his funds when he marries Jenny. They feel she is beneath him, that he could do better, and that their declaration of love is passing. Though they struggle without his father's money, they get by with Jenny working as a teacher. Unable to get pregnant, Jenny visits the doctor, who runs some tests and discovers that she is terminally ill. He tells Oliver, but Jenny finds out on her own.

Oliver goes to his father for money for Jenny's cancer treatment though he does not tell him that she is ill. His father asks if he has got a girl in trouble and gives his son enough for the abortion. Eventually, his father learns the truth and rushes to the hospital to find his son exiting the building. His father quickly stammers that he is sorry. Quoting his wife, who never held a grudge, Oliver says, "Love means never having to say you're sorry," and walks away alone.

O'Neal and MacGraw are wonderful as star-crossed lovers. Their charming banter and affection won us over, and we quickly fell for them. In any love story, you must believe the couple truly care for each other. We did with these two; they were perfectly cast. The narrative works nicely, and Ray Milland, as Oliver's smug and arrogant father, provides the perfect foil. John Marley (about to become famous in *The Godfather* as the movie producer who finds a horse head in his bed) is excellent as Jenny's father, who adores his hard-working daughter.

The film won a single Academy Award for its instantly recognizable musical score but was nominated for seven others, including Best Picture, Best Director, Best Actor, Best Actress, and Best Supporting Actor. Neither actor ever achieved the heights they did with this film, though O'Neal did work with Stanley Kubrick in *Barry Lyndon* (1975) and made a terrible sequel to *Love Story* entitled *Oliver's Story* (1977).

“Audiences openly wept as they exited the theatre, overcome by the film’s tragic ending.”

20

“Though *M*A*S*H* is set during the Korean War, make no mistake, this film is about the war in Vietnam.”

M*A*S*H (1970)

DIRECTED BY Robert Altman
COUNTRY USA

The acronym "MASH" in the US military stands for Mobile Ambulance Surgical Hospital. That fact helps us to appreciate both the comedy and drama in this film. Often surrounded by intense combat, the medical staff must work under such conditions, sewing bodies back together when they arrive by chopper.

Though *M*A*S*H* is set during the Korean War, make no mistake, this film is about the war in Vietnam. Hollywood reasoned it was too soon to make films about Vietnam because audiences weren't ready to watch them. It was still raging and wildly unpopular, so basing the movie there would mean courting a box office bomb. Unable to make his film about the ongoing conflict in Vietnam, Altman cleverly disguised it. The setting is Korea, but the movie looks like 1970. The characters have long hair, like the youth of the time, and wear badges popular during the war in Vietnam, such as "King Kong Died for our Sins."

Shocking at the time in its depiction of surgical work in the field, the movie was relentless in its honesty and authenticity but also managed to be very funny. Needing a break from the darkness of their lives, the doctors and nurses achieve it through comedy. To make their downtime bearable, they relentlessly torment their adversaries in the camp, exchange sarcastic quips, ferment booze, smoke pot, and play football, all distractions while they wait for the next sound of incoming helicopters. Throughout it all, the characters dream of home.

The two main troublemakers are surgeons Hawkeye Pierce (Donald Sutherland) and Trapper John McIntyre (Elliott Gould), who wreak havoc on the officious Major Burns (Robert Duvall). Only Major Houlihan/Hot Lips (Sally Kellerman) can stomach him. Eventually, their torrid affair is exposed brilliantly. Burns is carted off to the mental hospital, and Hawkeye and Trapper John win that battle of wits.

Robert Altman's film felt very new. Dialogue overlapped as characters talked over each other, just like in real life, and it was often dark and unpleasant in its depiction of war from the perspective of the people who tried to fix the human damage. It felt as if Altman had plonked a camera down in the middle of a war. Considering Vietnam was raging, and the other major war film that year was *Patton* (1970), Altman's film could not have been more divisive to audiences and critics, who responded by making the film a success.

When the nominations came out, there were some howling protests when the Academy nominations included neither Sutherland nor Gould. However, the movie was nominated for Best Picture, Best Director, Best Screenplay, Best Supporting Actress (Kellerman), and Best Film Editing. It would win Best Screenplay and the Golden Globe for Best Picture (Comedy/ Musical), and Altman was a Directors Guild nominee.

*M*A*S*H* remains one of the finest black comedies of the decade and made its director a star among filmmakers. A television series came out a couple of years later, which ran for eleven years, longer than the war in Korea. The series made it clear the setting was Korea, and there were no veiled comments about the war in Vietnam. It won many Emmy Awards and was among the first TV shows to kill off leading characters.

Opposite McIntyre (Elliott Gould) and Pierce (Donald Sutherland) enjoy a little downtime.

22 PATTON (1970)

DIRECTED BY Franklin J. Schaffner
COUNTRY USA

Opposite It's hard to imagine anyone but George C. Scott in this role.

Academy Award-winning actors Burt Lancaster, Lee Marvin, Rod Steiger, and John Wayne all turned down the role of General George S. Patton in the long-awaited biography of the hugely controversial general of the Second World War. Steiger later called his refusal of the role the "greatest regret of my career" after seeing the film.

The magnificent, towering performance of George C. Scott as Patton is at the centre of this powerful war biography. He is flawless, an astonishing piece of acting that stunned audiences and critics with its genius. A well-known and mightily respected character actor, Scott had given an array of great performances on screen and stage, but with *Patton*, he found the film that would allow him to create one for the ages.

From that iconic speech given in front of a massive American flag, which sets the tone for the film and the character, Scott inhabits Patton in every possible way. Patton was well known for being fearless, believing his courage inspired his men. He had no patience for anything less than unwavering determination among his men. When he famously slapped a man for breaking down in tears in front of him, the army took him to task. Though he apologized, did he mean it? Given his arrogance, maybe not.

Patton was a complicated man, a military genius who designed offensive campaigns and executed them without approval from his commanders. Even generals have superiors, but Patton often did not defer to his. He loved war, though he understood the cost. Ironically, it made him feel safe. He was a devout believer in reincarnation and often found places in Europe he believed he had been before as a warrior in a previous life.

Scott won the New York Film Critics Award as Best Actor and later won one of the film's seven Academy Awards for Best Actor, famously refusing to accept because he did not believe in the Academy Awards. Scott felt the New York Film Critics were the conscience of the American film industry and deemed them the only award worth accepting. The movie took home Oscars for Best Picture, Best Director, and the fine screenplay by Francis Ford Coppola and Edmund North. Coppola found a way into the story that had baffled many other writers.

In 1970, Vietnam was raging, the most unpopular war in the history of the United States. It was a year after the peaceful protests at Woodstock, and despite the war being so detested by the nation's youth, two of the year's most popular films were war pictures. The first being *Patton*, obviously, and the second was *M*A*S*H* (1970), set in Korea but relevant to Vietnam.

Patton brilliantly explores the contradictions of one of America's greatest generals, who was often in trouble for his brash arrogance despite being a brilliant leader. He could have become another Eisenhower, but his actions were often careless, and he alienated too many people in high places. Scott fearlessly portrays this, warts and all, in one of the great screen biographies.

A single performance rarely elevates a film to such lofty heights, but from the opening through to the final shot, your eyes will never leave the genius of George C. Scott. As Patton, he is miraculous.

"George C. Scott is flawless, an astonishing piece of acting that stunned audiences and critics with its genius."

24 "Truffaut made films about humanity, the good and bad of it."

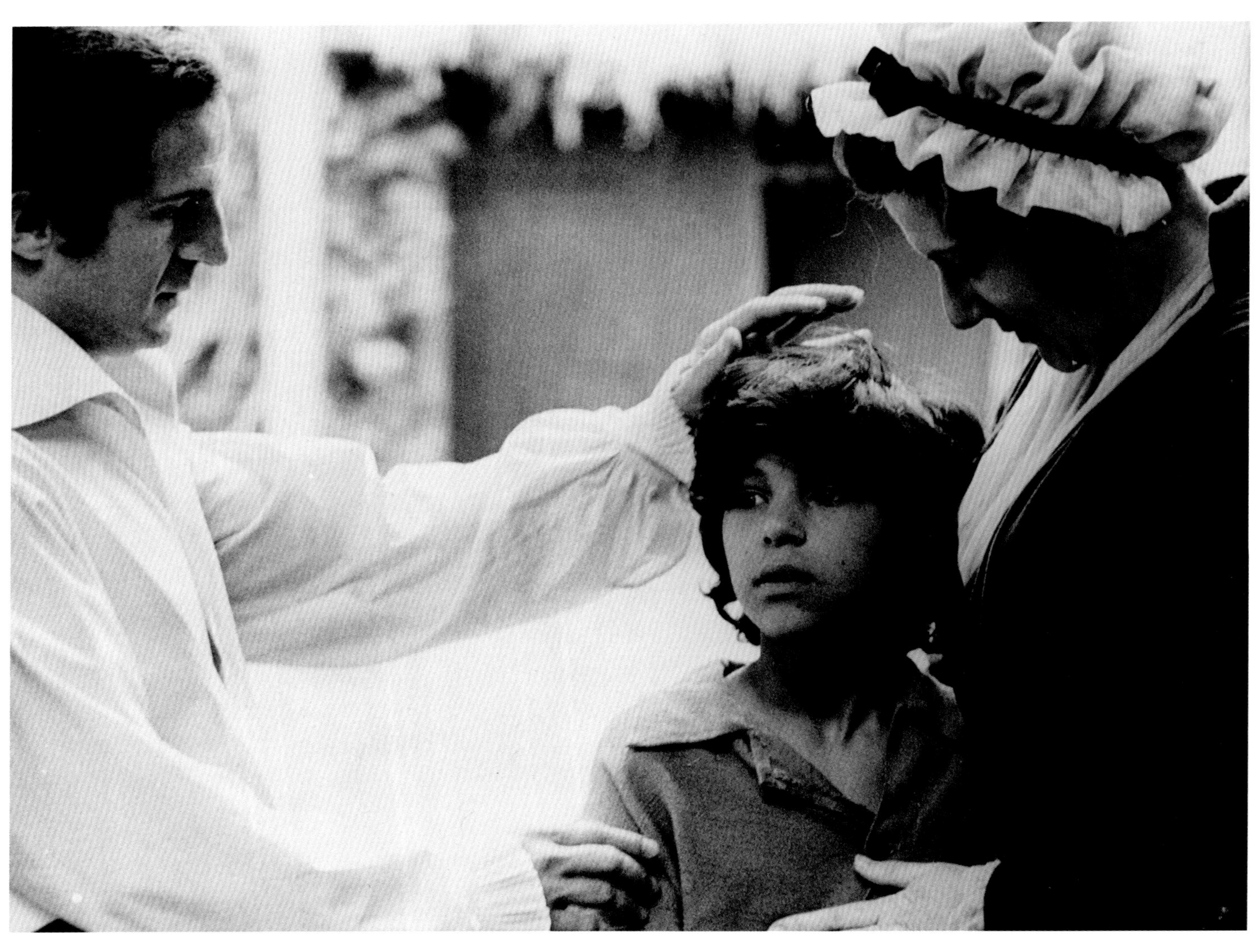

THE WILD CHILD (1970)

DIRECTED BY François Truffaut
COUNTRY France

The father of the French New Wave was said to be Jean-Luc Godard, who famously stated that all he needed to make a narrative film "was a guy, a girl, and a gun." There is no questioning the breakthroughs Godard made in cinema art, but I have always believed the most talented director of the time was François Truffaut, who gifted the world with one masterpiece after another. More so than Godard, who was more interested in experimental films, Truffaut made films about humanity, the good and bad of it. One of his finest films was his first of the 70s, *The Wild Child*.

The film opens with a statement telling the audience it is based on a true story that began in 1798 in a French forest.

A young boy is seen lumbering through the forest, and experts are dispatched to track down the child. They discover the boy has been living in the woods, surviving by his sheer wits for years. No one can say how long he has been alone in the dense forests, and because he doesn't speak, he cannot shed any light on the matter. He is, by all accounts, a wild animal, bearing no real signs of ever being civilized. The boy is finally captured and taken to Dr. Itard (Truffaut), who examines him and begins an integration into society. The boy is initially thought to be deaf, but the good doctor discovers he can hear fine , with the potential to be educated. But it will be a challenging task. Covered in scars from conflicts with other wild animals, the boy has grown into a fierce hunter unafraid to fight for his "turf."

The movie raises several questions about child-rearing, education, civilized society, and whether the child was better off wild in the forests. Will he ever belong? What will society give him that he could not have had in the woods? Indeed, a longer, more productive life, but will he ever be happier?

The boy, named Victor (Jean-Pierre Cargol), fights him every step of the way, though he does attempt to communicate. Slowly, the boy lets the doctor in; trust is earned over time. It is reminiscent of the mighty battle Annie Sullivan went through with Helen Keller, who could not see or hear her.

By the end of the story, the boy has picked up the beginnings of rudimentary language, and we have hope for him.

Truffaut, a gifted filmmaker, proved to be an equally good actor, particularly for Steven Spielberg in the miraculous *Close Encounters of the Third Kind* (1977). He is superb as Dr. Itard, as he and young Cargol have remarkable, believable chemistry. Watching their evolution through the film—every word, gesture, glance—feels authentic.

The film won awards for Best Foreign Language Film and Best Director from the National Board of Review and Best Cinematography from the National Society of Film Critics. The Academy curiously ignored it entirely.

Opposite Dr. Itard and Madame Guérin reassure Victor.

“What transpired has become known as one of America’s most memorable cultural events.”

WOODSTOCK (1970)

DIRECTED BY Michael Wadleigh
COUNTRY USA

It doesn't matter if you were alive in 1969. If asked to name the most renowned rock concert in history, Woodstock will likely come to mind. The legend of the three incredible days, with crowds of more than 400,000 gathered on Max Yasgur's farm in upstate New York, has withstood the test of time. Though it came together haphazardly, what transpired has become known as one of America's most memorable cultural events.

Watching the superb documentary Michael Wadleigh created with multiple cameras and an ocean of footage superbly cut together by a team of film editors, including Thelma Schoonmaker and a young Martin Scorsese, you feel like you are right there. We get to experience the musical performances but also witness the mud, the pond used for bathing, the washroom queues, and the food vendors scrambling to feed the masses.

The town's people were incredibly generous with the crowds of young people, making sure they were safe, that they ate ("the kids are hungry, you gotta' feed them"), and received medical attention when needed, usually for drug overdoses. There was no crime; it stayed true to its promise—a concert of peace, love, and music. The smiles of the young people enjoying themselves are infectious; we are witnessing true joy.

Traffic into the town stopped as people abandoned their cars on the New York interstate. Some of the acts had to hire helicopters to get access. Initially, the organizers anticipated 50,000 but nearly ten times that showed up to what became an accidental free concert.

And the music.

From Richie Havens opening the concert with "Handsome Johnny" to the end and Jimi Hendrix's astonishing "Star-Spangled Banner" on his guitar, audiences were mesmerized. The performers had their challenges. The wooden stage was slippery, so falling was a risk, and the rain led to electric shocks for anyone touching a microphone. But they persevered.

The film was a masterpiece of narrative, starting and placing everything in chronological order, beginning before the festival. The director uses split screens to show the complexity of the event; shots reveal an ocean of people on the farmland, while other cameras superbly catch the acts in their raw, visceral glory.

Woodstock won the Academy Award for Best Feature Documentary and nominations for Best Sound, but it also deserved nominations for Best Cinematography, Best Film Editing, and Best Picture. It is often hailed as the most outstanding documentary ever made. It very well might be.

Opposite The footage captured over the three days makes us feel like we are there.

28 A CLOCKWORK ORANGE (1971)

DIRECTED BY Stanley Kubrick
COUNTRY USA/United Kingdom

Opposite McDowell managed to be terrifying and mesmerizing at the same time.

The genius of Stanley Kubrick's dystopian *A Clockwork Orange*, made over fifty years ago, is that the future depicted here still seems plausible today. Such a visionary was this director. How does one define this film? Is it dark drama, satire, science fiction, or a vicious black comedy? Or is it all four?

Based on the book by Anthony Burgess, Kubrick insisted on keeping Burgess's slang from the book, a mix of English and Russian. Most of this dialect comes from Alex (Malcolm McDowell) and his *droogs* (gang), who terrorize the night, beating, stealing, raping, and eventually murdering.

We first encounter Alex, a Beethoven-obsessed young hoodlum, as he gives the audience a baleful stare in a bar, sitting with his three droogs drinking a concoction he calls milk-plus. They leave the bar and enter the night to wreak havoc on whomever they encounter. They beat an old homeless man unconscious, start a fight with another gang, and steal a car. In a frightening scene, they burst in on a writer and his wife, beat the man, and make him watch as they rape his wife. Alex places a ball in her mouth and winds tape around her head, dancing a soft shoe to "Singin' in the Rain." The droogs have their fun, destroy lives, and go home for the night.

But there is unrest in the group on several fronts. During a walk, Alex viciously lashes out at the group, sending them into the canal. This leads to the betrayal, where one of them smashes Alex in the face with a milk bottle after he murders a woman in her home. Alex is unable to escape from the police.

Sent to prison for murder, he volunteers to be a subject of the Ludovico treatment, an aversion therapy that uses non-stop images of violence to deter the prisoner from performing such acts. With his eyes propped open, and Beethoven at top volume, Alex endures this experiment for several days. If the treatment is successful, he will become physically ill if he even thinks of committing a crime (or hear Beethoven—a small side-effect).

Although he is declared "rehabilitated" and released, Alex is still a societal pariah. His parents have rented his room to a lovely young man, and a group of men attacks him, recognizing him as the one who beat their friend on the street. His three droogs have become police officers, encounter Alex, and give him a sound beating.

Alex winds up in the home of the writer. We learn that his wife died from the injuries inflicted by Alex. The writer, genuinely concerned, takes him in, clothes him, feeds him, and offers him a warm bath. While in the tub, Alex begins to hum "Singin' in the Rain," the song growing louder as the old man listens outside the door. He forces Alex into a locked attic and blasts Beethoven into the room until Alex jumps out of a window hoping for death. Instead, he is hurt terribly but becomes front-page news as the victim of government-sponsored torture. With a cruel smile, Alex dreams of an orgy and lets us know he is back.

Malcolm McDowell is astonishing as Alex, creating a funny, intriguing but cruel young hoodlum. He is the kind of monster who would kick a kitten as he walked past or feed it to his snake. Yet it is to McDowell's absolute credit that he makes us feel sorry for Alex during the experiments and after he gets out of prison. His power of choice is gone, taken away by the experiments. This would have been a much less powerful film, even with Kubrick's talent, without McDowell.

Banned in Britain for years, the film received an X-rating in North America and earned rave reviews. The New York Film Critics named it their best film of the year and awarded Kubrick their Best Director award. In addition, he received director nominations from the Directors Guild of America and the Academy. Inexplicably, McDowell was snubbed. The fact that the film is still discussed and revered rests solely on his performance.

“How does one define this film? Is it dark drama, satire, science fiction, or a vicious black comedy?”

"Nicholson is extraordinary as Jonathan, a misogynistic man who hates women for how they make him feel about himself."

CARNAL KNOWLEDGE (1971)

DIRECTED BY Mike Nichols
COUNTRY USA

Misogyny was never better explored than in Mike Nichols's cringe-worthy *Carnal Knowledge*, in which Jack Nicholson portrays a savage, sleazy womanizer without a care for anyone's feelings but his own. The hurt and pain he causes in each relationship mean nothing to him; he simply moves on. It might be the most disagreeable character Nicholson has ever portrayed. In a questionable bit of casting, singer Art Garfunkel plays Nicholson's best friend, and though he is adequate in the role, he does not reach the heights the other actors do.

Spanning thirty years, teenagers Jonathan (Nicholson) and Sandy (Garfunkel) meet in the 40s while attending Amherst College. The Second World War has ended, and hope governs the nation once again. Like most college students, their libido is in overdrive, so the topic of conversation often turns to women. Sandy worships women and is shy and polite around them, whereas Jonathan objectifies the opposite sex and is aggressive, like a dog in heat. The two men become best friends despite the fact they are so radically different.

The film follows the men into middle age, where we see the many failures in their lives with women. Jonathan is entirely about himself; he does not care if his partner is satisfied sexually or not, so long as he is. Boiled down to its core, the film is a study of the sexual lives of the two men, an aggressive Don Juan with both success and failure with women, and the shy, reserved Sandy, with more failures than successes, but he is at least decent and kind.

Nicholson is extraordinary as Jonathan, a misogynistic man who hates women for how they make him feel about himself. His success with women is how he measures his self-esteem. Garfunkel does not have the acting skills to create a full-bodied character as Nicholson does, but he is good enough to carry the part. Ann-Margret is a revelation as the woman of Nicholson's dreams whom he berates and slowly ruins. Though she tries, nothing this poor soul does is good enough for Jonathan. He belittles her constantly. Candice Bergen is outstanding as the girl Sandy falls for, and Jonathan cannot help but seduce, accidentally revealing this to his friend in the last few frames of the film.

Mike Nichols directed and, as always, drew fine performances from his actors. The characters here are often toxic; the actors courageously make them real. The director explores college as a breeding ground for sexual experimentation, a bold statement indeed.

Reviews were mixed, owing partially to the tricky subject matter. Nicholson's horrific treatment of Bobbie (Ann-Margret) was difficult for audiences to watch, impacting the film's box office.

Ann-Margret was nominated for an Academy Award as Best Supporting Actress, the film's only nomination.

Opposite Ann-Margret and Nicholson in one of several bedroom scenes.

32 **DIRTY HARRY** (1971)

DIRECTED BY Don Siegel
COUNTRY USA

Opposite Eastwood plays the steely-eyed, fearless Callahan.

Plenty of movies had portrayed the "cop who played by his own rules" by the time *Dirty Harry* made it to the screen in 1971. Still, audiences had never seen anyone like Harry Callahan. Known as "Dirty" Harry to those in the police department, he breaks all the rules but gets the criminals off the streets. His methods are odd, even dangerous, but they work.

John Wayne, Dean Martin, Frank Sinatra, and Jackie Gleason all got the call for the part, turned it down, and later regretted it. Warner Brothers finally offered it to Eastwood, who had made a name for himself with the spaghetti westerns he had made in Italy.

Dirty Harry sent him into the stratosphere, the world's leading box office attraction.

The narrative of *Dirty Harry* borrowed from the real-life Zodiac killer, who at this time was terrorizing California with a series of murders and then taunting the police. In the movie, the killer is Scorpio, portrayed brilliantly by Andy Robinson, a little-known character actor. He is ruthless, including children among his victims. In fact, children are his preferred targets. Harry is assigned the case and does indeed find the killer. But Harry is set up, and the killer goes to the police charging Harry with police brutality after being beaten by the cop.

We have seen Harry in action with his trusty .44 Magnum. Holding his target at gunpoint, he explains, "the .44 Magnum is the most powerful handgun in the world and will blow your head clean off." His targets typically make the wise choice to surrender.

Harry tracks Scorpio and eventually corners him, though the killer holds a young boy in front of him as a shield. Undeterred, Harry shoots him in the shoulder, the boy bolts, and Harry kills him at last.

Audiences seemed to love the film much more than critics, who enjoyed Eastwood's performance, but the film was not worthy of awards. No matter: in thirty years, Eastwood would get his crack at the Academy Awards and twice dominate them.

Dirty Harry was our introduction to the stoic, steely-eyed, fearless Callahan. Eastwood was a very limited actor at this point in his career, not having grown into the excellent actor he became later in life. Andy Robinson is superb as the killer, genuinely terrifying and just the sort of character audiences love to hate.

The film began a long relationship with Don Siegel, who taught Eastwood about the art of directing. Eastwood dedicated his first movie to Siegel. While better films of this sort were made through the 70s and beyond, the success of the *Dirty Harry* franchise gave Eastwood leverage to negotiate an opportunity to direct movies of his own, launching his second career.

"John Wayne, Dean Martin, Frank Sinatra, and Jackie Gleason all got the call for the part, turned it down, and later regretted it."

34

"A strange little black comedy that has become arguably the preeminent cult film of the decade."

HAROLD AND MAUDE (1971)

DIRECTED BY Hal Ashby
COUNTRY USA

Hal Ashby has four films in this book alongside Francis Ford Coppola, who basically owned the 70s with his output of great films. He is lesser known than Coppola, often overlooked for his astonishing array of work, but no less substantial. The quiet, anti-authoritarian Ashby began his career as a film editor, winning an Academy Award for *In the Heat of the Night* (1967) for his friend and mentor, Norman Jewison. Soon after, Jewison chose Ashby to direct *The Landlord* (1970). Though not groundbreaking, it was a solid piece of filmmaking, and Ashby transitioned to directing (though he continued to cut his own films).

His second film was *Harold and Maude*, a strange little black comedy that has become arguably the preeminent cult film of the decade.

Harold (Bud Cort) is a depressed young man from a wealthy family. He is obsessed with death, attending funerals for strangers, driving a hearse, and staging mock suicides to shock his mother. It never works. Partly because she is on to him and partly because she is bored with his foolish behaviour. Then he meets Maude (Ruth Gordon), a seventy-nine-year-old free spirit who alters the course of his life. Maude believes in living each day as if it is her last. Befriending the morose Harold, she teaches him how to enjoy life, and Harold begins to fall in love with her. During one of their outings, Harold notices, to his horror, the tattoo of a holocaust survivor on Maude's wrist. He realizes she doesn't fear death; she has already escaped it many times.

Announcing he will marry Maude, Harold sends his mother into a full-scale panic. She does everything to change his mind, setting him up with a long list of potential wives, but he and Maude thwart her every move. When Maude turns eighty, Harold throws her a party. As they dance, she tells him she has taken a bottle of sleeping pills and will be dead by midnight. Harold rushes Maude to the hospital, but she passes away, leaving him alone. He takes the expensive car his mother gifted him and sends it over a cliff before pulling out the banjo Maude taught him to play, strumming a tune in his uncharacteristically colourful outfit. Maude now lives within Harold, and her life force has saved him.

Ruth Gordon had just won a Best Supporting Actress Oscar for *Rosemary's Baby* (1968) when she was cast in this film, beating out some of the most formidable global talent at the time. No one else could have played the role so perfectly. Gordon's eyes dance with mischief but also with deep sadness. She has seen humanity at its worst and become a life force to beat back death. All these years later, it is still stunning to consider her name wasn't among the nominees for Best Actress. Her performance is the only one in 1971 that might have challenged Jane Fonda in *Klute*.

Bud Cort also beat out some impressive talent to play Harold, Richard Dreyfuss among them. His is a marvellous droll performance, taking his character from a dark, suicidal, hopeless figure to a reborn young man with his whole life ahead of him. Though he was also perfectly cast, he never enjoyed the career Ashby hoped for him.

Harold and Maude was a critical and box office flop when it opened, but with time, a curious thing happened: college campuses began to offer midnight screenings. The film slowly became a cult classic. By 1983, it had made a profit, and critics started to include it among their favourite movies of the 70s. The film demonstrated Ashby's gentle touch with actors, who adored working with him.

Opposite Harold and Maude at a funeral, sharing their love of all things death related.

36

"She did not open doors for women so much as kick them down, stomp on them, and walk through."

KLUTE (1971)

DIRECTED BY Alan J. Pakula
COUNTRY USA

Everything about Bree Daniels (Jane Fonda) tells us she is tough. A prostitute, arrogant, fearless, and confident in her sexuality, she is not one to back down from confrontation. But when she receives a phone call from her stalker, who plays a recorded conversation between her and a client, we see absolute terror on her face. All resolve and courage melt away. This might be the only time we see the real Bree, as she usually wears an emotional mask. There is a classic scene where she is with a client, making love, and in the throes of it, she checks her watch to ensure he gets only the time he paid for.

It was a few seconds of screen time but demonstrated Fonda's immense talent beautifully, firmly placing the actress in the upper echelon of the greats of the 70s.

Though Jane Fonda won many awards and accolades for her searing performance in *Klute*, has she ever been credited for altering the direction of performance art in the 70s? Marlon Brando, Jack Nicholson, and Robert De Niro all received due praise for their performances, but Fonda? Her work provided nothing less than a seismic event for film acting. She did not open doors for women so much as kick them down, stomp on them, and walk through.

Klute was among the first "women's films," and proudly so. Vivien Leigh had long ago declared that in the proper role, a woman could carry a film, even a three-hour picture like *Gone with the Wind* (1939), in which Leigh gave one of the most astounding performances as feisty, calculating Scarlett O'Hara. With relaxed rules about acceptable topics on screen, *Klute* freely explored sexuality, prostitution, and a woman's sense of vulnerability.

Fonda went a step further with her remarkable performance as Daniels, displaying a toughness merged with a vulnerability we had never seen before. It was a dark, uncompromising performance and a role that, up to that time, was usually assigned to men.

Interestingly, the name of the lead character is Bree Daniels, yet the film's title is *Klute* (Donald Sutherland), the name of the private investigator trying to protect her. So, while it may be a women's film, they weren't ready to make a complete leap.

The film is superbly directed by Alan J. Pakula, who captures Bree's growing sense of paranoia by simply letting Fonda do her thing in front of the camera. She dominates the film. Bree is very aware of her effect on men and often hates herself for it. Yet her relationship with Klute builds her self-esteem, and there is hope in her life by the end.

Fonda's performance was miraculous and remains so. She won everything an actress could win that year, the National Society of Film Critics Award, the New York Film Critics Circle Best Actress Award, the Golden Globe, and to her surprise, the Academy Award. Her anti-Vietnam activities made the Academy nervous, fearing she would make a political speech. Instead, they got a very classy Fonda accepting her award, thanking the Academy, and ending with: "There is a great deal to say, but I'm not going to say it tonight."

So much was made of Fonda, but little was said about sad-eyed Donald Sutherland, who was superb as Klute, along with steely Roy Scheider as Bree's dangerous pimp. Each was outstanding but the film belonged to Fonda.

The performance made her the leading actress of the 70s, at which point she made one other film, *Steelyard Blues* (1972), before walking away from Hollywood for five years.

Opposite Jane Fonda mastered the tough yet vulnerable persona in her role as Bree.

38 PLAY MISTY FOR ME (1971)

DIRECTED BY Clint Eastwood
COUNTRY USA

Opposite Eastwood was a busy man directing and editing this thriller.

Back in the 70s, no one could have guessed that Clint Eastwood would become one of the most artistic and formidable film directors in the business, with multiple Oscar nominations and four wins, two for Best Director, two for Best Picture. Along with the Oscars, *Unforgiven* (1992) and *Million Dollar Baby* (2004) both won DGA Awards, and he was nominated as Best Actor for both. Nominations also came for *Mystic River* (2003) and *Letters from Iwo Jima* (2006), and there were howls of protest when the Academy ignored his superb performance in *Gran Torino* (2008). One film, *American Sniper* (2014), was a Best Picture nominee, but strangely, Eastwood was ignored as the director.

He had to barter for his first chance at directing. Warner Brothers would let him direct if he agreed to act in another movie. That "one for them, one for you" arrangement continued for several years. Not a bad deal, as it turned out. *Play Misty for Me* delivered millions at the box office.

It was a thriller in the Hitchcock vein of films, filled with tension and mounting dread that worked on the audience. Eastwood portrays a Californian disc jockey who gets involved with a listener who calls in constantly asking him to "play 'Misty' for me," and he obliges. He meets her at a bar, not knowing she is the caller. He hits on her, takes her home, and only then does Evelyn (Jessica Walter) disclose her identity. They begin a casual relationship. Very quickly, Evelyn shows signs of being unbalanced. She demands his constant attention. He ends the relationship after she disrupts an important business meeting and makes a scene.

However, Evelyn will not let go. She hounds him, attempts suicide by slashing her wrists, and goes after the new love in his life. In the final scene, she tries to kill them both. In the struggle, he throws her out of a window, ultimately to her death.

If it sounds a bit familiar, the plot of *Fatal Attraction* (1987) was very similar.

Critics were very supportive of Eastwood's work. By 1976, Orson Welles was calling him "the finest director working in America." Through the 80s and into the 90s, he honed his skills into an art form. He had come a long way since the spaghetti westerns made him a star.

Actress Jessica Walter, making her lead debut, earned rave reviews and was nominated for a Golden Globe but sadly not an Oscar as they had hoped. She credited Eastwood for her performance, claiming he knew what to say and when to say it.

Although Eastwood had to battle for the chance to direct, Hollywood now regards him as one of the most influential directors of the past forty years.

"Although Eastwood had to battle for the chance to direct, Hollywood now regards him as one of the most influential directors of the past forty years."

"Truly a frightening tale, but a wild hallucinatory film. *The Devils* is a demanding cinematic experience."

THE DEVILS (1971)

DIRECTED BY Ken Russell
COUNTRY United Kingdom

Loosely based on Aldous Huxley's electrifying novel *The Devils of Loudun*, Ken Russell's *The Devils* might be the most infamous film to emerge from Britain in the last fifty years. The imagery and startling narrative stunned audiences into silence when the film first opened and left film critics unsure of what to write about. What could not be denied was the film's visceral, raw power, and the courageous performances of the actors, especially Oliver Reed and Vanessa Redgrave.

Russell was a fearless director and known to use wretched excess in his films. He often went wildly and unapologetically over the top. By 1971, he was a world-class filmmaker, having made both *Women in Love* (1970) and *The Music Lovers* (1970) the year before, and *The Boy Friend* (1971) came out just before *The Devils*. Russell had exploded into international cinema and *The Devils* made him famous.

The film explores with frenzied emotions the events surrounding a seventeenth-century priest Grandier (Oliver Reed), who goes to war against the Catholic Church and state for the independence of the small French town Loudun. Accused of witchcraft by a hunchback nun, Sister Jeanne (Vanessa Redgrave), the priest is tried and eventually burnt at the stake.

With so many wild scenes to choose from, the exorcism of the hunchback nun remains extraordinary for its manic energy and fury. Vanessa Redgrave might have done the finest work of her impressive career in *The Devils*. It is difficult to imagine a more fearless actress. Though the good sister is clearly sexually obsessed with the priest, she has no physical connection with him until given a bone from his burnt body, which she promptly masturbates with.

Oliver Reed was an underrated actor through the 60s and 70s, and this is arguably the finest performance of his career. He, Redgrave, and Russell are in lockstep throughout the film. Their combined work is magic.

Truly a frightening tale, but a wild hallucinatory film. *The Devils* is a demanding cinematic experience. The sex is portrayed with authenticity and honesty, and the burning of the priest is as horrific as I imagine a real burning must be. The flesh blisters, as the body is engulfed by the flames, truly one of the most frightening deaths committed to film.

The Devils went through so many edits, with crucial scenes cut, that it has become difficult to find a pure Russell cut. We owe it to the filmmaker to see the film he intended, for better or worse.

Opposite In one of the most bizarre and controversial films of the 70s, Oliver Reed gave a powerful performance as a charismatic priest.

42 THE FRENCH CONNECTION (1971)

DIRECTED BY William Friedkin
COUNTRY USA

Opposite A young Gene Hackman and Roy Scheider as two relentless cops.

Friedkin wanted *The French Connection* to have an authentic, gritty, almost documentary feel. He takes us into the world of narcotics detectives, following the real-life escapades of renegade cop Popeye Doyle (Gene Hackman). His rough and tumble partner Russo (Roy Scheider) is like-minded, making them a good team.

Popeye discovers that a wealthy drug dealer from France, Charnier (Fernando Rey), is in New York for a huge drug deal. It becomes Popeye's obsession. But Charnier is not a routine drug dealer; he's a drug lord who is not intimidated by American cops. In one memorable scene, he outwits Popeye on the subway and waves goodbye through the glass of the door. That wave is returned by Popeye when they finally have Charnier cornered. Incredibly, he escapes and heads back to France, where he is safe from the American police.

In making the film so realistic, Friedkin immerses audiences in this seedy world without apology. We see what the detectives go through, the endless waiting, stomping their feet to stay warm, drinking endless cups of stale coffee, having a lead come up empty, and the worst, losing their prey in the blink of an eye. We witness a car chase as Popeye pursues a subway train on the tracks above the street at top speeds. We watch breathlessly as he nearly hits bystanders, curses, and pounds his steering wheel. He eventually catches the criminal and shoots him dead as he tries to escape. It is a remarkable scene even today.

Gene Hackman became a major star after the film, winning an Oscar and the New York Film Critics Award for his performance. He plays Popeye as a tough, vulgar, fearless cop, not averse to slapping around criminals to get more information. He lives in a binary world with a clear right and wrong but doesn't mind bending the rules if it helps to finish a job. It was a landmark role for the actor.

Fernando Rey is superb as the gentleman criminal, the elegant and cultured Charnier, who happens to be a drug lord. And Roy Scheider (Oscar-nominated for Best Supporting Actor) as Russo, partner to Popeye, is excellent as well playing the haggard but dedicated cop. He and Hackman are a perfect match together.

The French Connection was nominated for eight Academy Awards and took home five, winning Best Picture, Best Actor, Best Director (Friedkin), Best Screenplay Adaptation, and Best Film Editing (the brilliant editing on the car chase alone would have been enough to win that one).

A sequel came four years later (*French Connection II* (1975)), and many critics believe Hackman's performance surpassed the original. The first remains a template for filmmakers hoping to create a believable crime film on the streets of New York. You can almost smell the exhaust.

"Friedkin immerses audiences into this seedy world without apology."

44 THE LAST PICTURE SHOW (1971)

DIRECTED BY Peter Bogdanovich
COUNTRY USA

Opposite Shepherd and Bridges both launched their career in this coming-of-age piece.

Small towns hold secrets, often profound and dark. Those living in these towns think they know everyone's business but do not. They would be shocked if they did.

Anarene, Texas, the tiny town in *The Last Picture Show*, is such a town, with one main street, a few shops, a diner that serves a popular hamburger, a billiard hall, and an old movie house. It is not much of a town except for those who live there; to them, it is home, with significance attached to every street corner.

Most of the film focuses on the exploits of two best friends just graduating high school, Duane (Jeff Bridges) and Sonny (Timothy Bottoms), who have known each other for years. Duane dates the prettiest girl in the town, Jacy (Cybill Shepherd), who is vain, spoiled, and full of herself. Her mother, Lois (Ellen Burstyn), worries (with reason) that her daughter will turn out exactly like her. Hellbent on losing her virginity, Jacy takes steps to make that happen, and after an unsuccessful trial run, she is no longer a virgin. Sonny breaks up with his high school girlfriend and has an affair with a middle-aged woman, Ruth (Cloris Leachman), the wife of the high school coach. Bored and deeply lonely, Ruth lights up when Sonny comes to see her.

The shocking and sudden death of the beloved and decent Sam (Ben Johnson) stuns them all. Sam was a fixture, owned half (or more) of the town, and dispensed wisdom to the younger boys, taking care especially of the mentally challenged Billy (Sam Bottoms), who spends his time sweeping the dust about on the streets. Secrets emerge about Sam and Lois, once an item and the great love of her life.

When the target of Jacy's scheming marries, she takes up with Sonny, bringing him and Duane to blows. She suggests the two run off and get married. Before she makes Sonny her latest love, she has sex with Abilene, her mother's lover, on top of a pool table. Though Jacy marries Sonny, they get pulled over by the police before they can consummate the marriage. It turns out Jacy alerted the police in the hopes they would be stopped before marrying. Her deceit knows no bounds. Her father bails her out but not Sonny, leaving it to Jacy's mother to bail him out. Realizing Ruth at least loved him, he returns to this poor broken woman who accepts him, but only after exploding at him in anger.

The town is rocked further by the accidental, tragic death of gentle Billy, hit by a truck as he swept his streets. Sonny realizes that Sam the Lion was the glue that held the town together. Sonny will take that mantle and do his best to provide what was missing without Sam: basic human decency.

There were howls of protest when *The Last Picture Show* came out, particularly over the skinny-dipping scene at the pool where the kids gather one evening. Full frontal nudity stunned viewers, but the film was still rated just R. The scene was an integral part of the narrative, demonstrating Jacy's need to be noticed, and it was in good taste.

The ensemble cast was superb, from the leading roles to the most minor supporting. Bogdanovich took a huge risk casting so many unknown young actors, but Bridges, Bottoms, and Shepherd were all superb. Bridges earned his first Academy Award nomination.

The veteran actors, however, were astounding. Ben Johnson did the best work of his long career as Sam, a good man trying to pass on some of that goodness. Cloris Leachman was brilliant as Ruth, the wounded wife of a closet homosexual, she finds love with a teenage boy. Ellen Burstyn proved her worthiness as an actress here as well, receiving her first nomination.

And Cybill Shepherd, confident, haughty, and sexy, was perfect as Jacy. Some said it was an easy role for her because she was playing herself. When asked to step outside this role in other films, she was a travesty and became best known as Bogdanovich's girlfriend. The two of them became infamous within Hollywood circles for their inflated egos. She quickly became, along with Bogdanovich, a pariah. Yet we can't deny that Bogdanovich created two of the greatest films of the decade, the other being *Paper Moon* (1973). Once more, he explored America's past, paying homage to the directors he admired during his career as a film critic.

The Last Picture Show was nominated for eight Academy Awards and won two for Ben Johnson and Cloris Leachman in their supporting roles. Johnson swept the major awards that year for Supporting Actor, and Leachman managed to win as well, though the New York Film Critics went with her co-star, Burstyn.

The film's black and white cinematography gave the film a haunting look, as though we were observing a past that no longer existed. There is no question Bogdanovich was a major talent brought down by ego, his own, making him the first casualty of the 70s caused by success.

46 AGUIRRE, THE WRATH OF GOD (1972)

DIRECTED BY Werner Herzog
COUNTRY Germany

Opposite Herzog created a claustrophobic feel with his brilliant cinematography.

Klaus Kinski was a force of nature, an electrifying actor whose intensity was often alarming to watch. You could not take your eyes off this man with the formidable glare; he was terrifying. He and Herzog had a long and fruitful creative relationship, though fraught with nasty fights. They often came to blows; the director reportedly threatened to shoot Kinski while in the jungles of South America. Kinski was later diagnosed with severe mental health issues. His daughter wrote that he abused and raped her during her childhood. For the most part, the actor hid these issues from his co-workers.

Aguirre, The Wrath of God influenced many films that followed but is most evident in Francis Ford Coppola's *Apocalypse Now* (1979). Both are quest films; both contain a journey on water; and death awaits them on the river. This film takes place in 1560 in Peru, where conquistadors roam the jungles searching for long-promised treasures. When Pizarro (Alejandro Repullés) hears of El Dorado's riches, he gathers a group of men and sends them on a flimsy raft down the Amazon to find the treasures. On the raft is Aguirre (Kinski), an unstable warrior who sees himself as the leader and the one man who can accomplish this mission.

Entirely deluded, Aguirre is a danger to them all. One by one, the natives hiding in the jungle at the river's edge kill the men on the raft, throwing darts with poison tips or spears. The raft becomes overrun with spider monkeys (which really happened during production). Eventually, no one is left but Aguirre, who promises to show whoever challenges him the wrath of God.

Set almost entirely on a raft, the film has a claustrophobic feeling for the audience as the narrative progresses. Surrounded by a lush, unforgiving jungle and endless river ahead, there is nowhere to go, which works emotionally on each of them in different ways. Aguirre was likely mad before they launched, but the closeness, the deaths of his companions, the dangers lurking so close in the jungles, and the constant threat of attack on the raft have driven him to worse heights of megalomania. By the end, he has only the monkeys to command. How much longer can he last on the raft?

The film was shot on location in Peru, with not nearly enough money, but the actors and crew believed in Herzog and Kinski (despite what they heard and saw). Somehow, Herzog emerged from the jungle with a work of art, surprising even himself. The film's cinematography is utterly breathtaking, and Herzog permitted effects of the elements to remain—water on the lenses, sun flashes in the camera, all of which give the film a greater sense of realism. The film feels like, through some miracle, it was produced in 1560 and captured hell unfolding on this raft.

Kinski is truly remarkable in the film, as we watch him descend into madness, though knowing as much about the production as we do, was he acting? A troubling masterpiece from the New German Cinema.

“Somehow Herzog emerged from the jungle with a work of art, surprising even himself.”

48

“Bergman’s *Cries and Whispers* can lay claim to being among the finest films ever made.”

CRIES AND WHISPERS (1972)

DIRECTED BY Ingmar Bergman
COUNTRY Sweden

Like *The Godfather* (1972), *The Godfather Part II* (1974), and many other films in this book, Ingmar Bergman's *Cries and Whispers* can lay claim to being among the finest films ever made.

By 1972, Bergman was a master filmmaker, probably the finest in Europe, and had earned the freedom to make whatever movie he chose. While his films are often bleak studies of humanity, they are powerfully realistic works, superbly acted and written (by Bergman). His work influenced generations of directors, Woody Allen, Hal Ashby, and Martin Scorsese among them.

In the house she grew up in, Agnes (Harriet Andersson) is dying, nursed by her two sisters, Karin (Ingrid Thulin) and Maria (Liv Ullmann). The sisters have long repressed their emotions, which has not changed since their return to their home, as they face imminent death with silent cries and whispers. So great and intense is their emotional distance that the sisters barely touch one another. The house is blanketed in sadness and stillness as they wait patiently for Agnes to pass on.

After Agnes dies, the sisters experience vivid dreams, and old memories come back to haunt them. Though gone from their lives, Agnes seems more alive than ever. Her appearance in their dreams helps the surviving sisters mend their differences and unite, though only fleetingly. As in real life, they can't solve their family trauma so easily and are soon back to their old ways. Their treatment of Anna, the maid who loved Agnes, is dreadful.

Bergman's use of colour in the film is bold and daring, similar to Spielberg's *Schindler's List* (1993) twenty years later. The fade to red means so much more when we learn of the self-mutilation and violence the sisters have in their pasts.

Like a fine stage ensemble, the acting is uniformly excellent, though Ullmann does stand out because she was, along with Jane Fonda, the most outstanding screen actress of her time. Ullmann had the innate ability to convey and say so much in stillness, without moving a muscle, only through her eyes. She was an astonishing actress. Thulin and Andersson are superb, and together they create one of the best screen-acting trios ever assembled.

Today, Ingmar Bergman is often forgotten, which is to our eternal shame because this man was an artist of the highest order who understood cinema as few directors ever have. Like Kubrick, he insisted his audiences not just watch the film but experience it. He took risks to be sure and, with those risks, challenged his audiences to look deeper, to go into the minds of the characters.

Cries and Whispers was nominated for five Academy Awards, including Best Picture, Best Director, and Best Cinematography, which it won.

The film remains Bergman's masterpiece.

Opposite Bergman's use of colour in the film is bold and daring.

50 DELIVERANCE (1972)

DIRECTED BY John Boorman
COUNTRY USA

Opposite Reynolds proved his broad acting range in this haunting tale.

One of the most terrifying films ever made is John Boorman's *Deliverance*, a multiple Oscar nominee and critically acclaimed box office hit. I first saw the film when I was only thirteen years old, and a man raping another man was alien to me. It was a long time before I could even speak about the film but finally I did with my father, who wisely decided to take me to see it again.

On the way home, he described what rape was and that, yes, it could happen to a man. He explained that rape was not an act of sex, but violence meant to dehumanize the victim. That was certainly what happened in the film, and it was horrifying.

This bold, unsettling film is about a group of friends from the city who go backwater canoeing down a river in a valley about to become flooded through the building of a dam. These are the Georgia backwoods, very backward and far from society. Some of the people they encounter in these hills are indeed hillbillies, uneducated, many born of incest, so living with severe disabilities. Lewis (Burt Reynolds) accepts the people for what they are, while Bobby (Ned Beatty) makes fun of them, displaying a nasty streak the others do not share. Ed (Jon Voight) admires Lewis as a fearless warrior, the kind of man you want with you on an adventure. Drew (Ronny Cox) is the smiling musician of the group, trying to live his life by a moral code of honesty.

The first day goes well as they make their way down the river, though Lewis does not care for Bobby. The next day, Bobby and Ed come across two men who take them into the woods at gunpoint. Bobby is raped and made to squeal like a pig. Ed is forced to watch, a belt around his neck holding him tight. The other man is about to force Ed to perform oral sex on him when Ed's eyes widen, and we see what he sees. Lewis, with his bow and arrow, poised and ready to shoot. His arrow pierces the chest of the man who raped Bobby. The other rushes into the woods.

They now have a dilemma—do they tell the authorities they have killed a man? True, that man had raped their friend, but does Bobby want this getting out? Do any of them? Drew insists the right thing to do is call the police when they get downriver but gets overruled by the others. They dispose of the body and are on the lookout for the other man as they make their way downriver. More disaster strikes. Drew's fate is unknown at this point and Lewis is injured when his canoe flips over, shattering his leg against the rock. It is left to Ed to scale the rocks high above the water and kill the man who managed to get away.

Back in the town, the men are in terrible condition, but Lewis lets them know he told the police nothing. The local sheriff knows something is off with their story, but he cannot prove it. He makes clear to them they should not ever do anything like this again. The men return to their city lives, Ed haunted by dreams of being on the river, seeing Drew's stiff body coming to the surface.

Burt Reynolds gave a powerful performance as Lewis, a superb macho piece of acting that goes from being the most powerful of the men to being reduced to a screaming mess of pain in a canoe. As Ed, Jon Voight reveals inner strength, ultimately saving the men. Ronny Cox makes a quiet impression as Drew. After his death, the men declare, "he was the best of us." Ned Beatty, in a fearless performance, is excellent as the smug, selfish Bobby. How much will the men be altered after their deliverance from this weekend journey?

Although the Academy snubbed the actors entirely, John Boorman and the film were deservedly nominated. The film became famous for a lyrical sequence in which Drew plays guitar with a young man, likely the victim of incest, who plays a mean banjo. They go toe to toe with one another until the boy leaves Drew in the dust. It is a magical sequence in a film filled with horrors.

It remains one of the most haunting films ever made.

"How much will the men be altered after their deliverance from this weekend journey?"

“Pollack captures the rugged beauty of the land in the film, the cinematography pristine and stunning.”

JEREMIAH JOHNSON (1972)

DIRECTED BY Sydney Pollack
COUNTRY USA

Robert Redford was never a great actor. He was good, no question, but never in the same league as Marlon Brando or his friend Paul Newman. Redford excelled in romantic comedy or portraying the flawed all-American man. He knew his limitations and chose his roles accordingly. Over his impressive acting career, before he turned to directing, three performances stood out. The first was as the deadly gunfighter in *Butch Cassidy and the Sundance Kid* (1969), and the second was as Hubbell Gardiner, an aspiring writer who sells out to Hollywood in the romantic hit *The Way We Were* (1973). He and Barbra Streisand were magical together and, with help from Sydney Pollack, created one of the screen's greatest love stories.

But his best work, in a film that elevated him to another level, was *Jeremiah Johnson*. The film tells the story of mountain man John Johnson, a hermit who resided in the Rocky Mountains in the mid-1800s. We follow his life as he finds his place among nature in the majestic mountains, finding a family when he is gifted a native woman as a bride and adopts a young boy. The Crow tribe massacres his family, and he dedicates his life to seeking revenge. He proves to be a fierce and resourceful warrior against the Crow tribe, cutting them down one by one before disappearing into what we hope is a peaceful life in the wild.

Redford commands the screen, his presence particularly powerful because he does not say much throughout the film. He relies on his body language and facial expressions to tell the story. Few performances have managed to say so much with so little.

Pollack captures the rugged beauty of the land in the film, the cinematography pristine and stunning. He and Redford have always worked in sync, and their trusting relationship serves the movie well.

Will Geer, who became famous playing the grandfather on the hit TV drama *The Waltons*, has a small but vital role as an old trapper who advises Johnson. But for most of the film, it is just Redford doing all the work. He beautifully captures the anguish of losing his wife and son, a void he never manages to fill for the rest of his life.

Granted, 1972 was a strong year for actors, but regardless, the Academy should have found room for Redford among the five Best Actor nominees. His performance was among the year's very best. Audiences loved the film, making it a surprise hit, and critics lavished praise on both the picture and Redford. Though he has a long career of excellence, he never matched the brilliant performance of this film.

Opposite The rugged landscape is its own character in this film along with Robert Redford and Will Geer.

INTERMISSION: FRANCIS FORD COPPOLA

Has an American filmmaker ever dominated a decade in the manner Francis Ford Coppola dominated the 70s? An argument could certainly be made for Elia Kazan in the 50s, though as impressive as Kazan's work was, it does not hold up against Coppola's.

He directed *The Godfather* (1972), which won the Academy Award as Best Picture, *The Conversation* (1974), a Best Picture nominee, *The Godfather Part II* (1974), a Best Picture and Best Director winner, and *Apocalypse Now* (1979), again a nominee for Best Picture. He won the Directors Guild of America Award for *The Godfather* and *The Godfather Part II* and was nominated for *The Conversation* and *Apocalypse Now*. The four films he directed are among the decade's finest, easily in the top fifteen.

Upon release, *The Godfather* was declared the greatest American film since *Citizen Kane* (1941), and just two years later, most agreed its sequel surpassed the original. Many, this critic included, consider *The Godfather Part II* the best American film ever.

He produced for his friend George Lucas *American Graffiti* (1973), which became a huge box office hit, was nominated for five Academy Awards, including Best Picture, and would usher in a nostalgia craze for music and clothing from the 50s and 60s that spilled over into television.

Coppola won three Academy Awards for writing the screenplays for *Patton* (1970), *The Godfather*, and *The Godfather Part II,* along with nominations for *The Conversation* and *Apocalypse Now*. In addition, he wrote the screenplay to *The Great Gatsby* (1974), a box office and critical failure, though the script was fiercely loyal to the book.

And if that were not enough, he created a film studio, American Zoetrope, dedicated to the new emerging filmmaker, where they could make their films for budgets of $1 million or less, free of interference of any kind from profit-obsessed studios.

Coppola was, if you will permit me, the Godfather of the New American Cinema, surrounded by gifted new directors he protected and would champion to the studios. He was unique, emotional, and fearless, refusing to back down from the studios even if his job was on the line. When Universal Pictures announced they were unimpressed with *American Graffiti* upon their first screening, Coppola whipped out his chequebook and offered to buy the film from them and distribute it himself. Sensing that the gifted director of *The Godfather* must see something in the film, Universal kept it and released it on their own, reaping the profits for the work, but losing Lucas in the process, who went on to make *Star Wars* for 20th Century Fox.

After *The Godfather Part II* won six Academy Awards, Coppola packed up his family and headed for the

Above Coppola with his two stars in *The Godfather Part II*, Marlon Brando and Al Pacino.

Philippines to make the first major American film about Vietnam. *Apocalypse Now* was fraught with troubles, such as replacing star Harvey Keitel after a week's shooting with Martin Sheen, then dealing with Sheen's subsequent near-fatal massive heart attack. But Coppola just carried on shooting. Typhoons wiped out his sets; the helicopters on loan from the Philippine military would routinely be called away in the middle of a shot to fight the rebels in the nearby hills; the heat was insufferable, and the rain came down with a pelting force. Dennis Hopper was so wired on drugs he was barely coherent, and then Marlon Brando arrived, hugely overweight and not having bothered to learn his lines. He and Coppola huddled together most days to discuss the character of Kurtz, rarely getting much done.

Yet somehow, he created a masterpiece.

In 1979, he took the film as a work in progress to the Cannes Film Festival, received a seventeen-minute standing ovation, and won the Palme d'Or, the festival's top prize. He brashly declared, "my film is not about Vietnam; my film is Vietnam." The accolades have continued to rain down on the film since that day so long ago.

In the years since, Coppola has never again enjoyed the success he had in the 70s, though he has been quite active. Given the fortune his wine empire has earned, he never needs money from a studio again.

"Coppola was unique, emotional, and fearless, refusing to back down from the studios even if his job was on the line."

56 THE COWBOYS (1972)

DIRECTED BY Mark Rydell
COUNTRY USA

Opposite John Wayne as Andersen with one of his young apprentices.

Having won his long overdue Academy Award for Best Actor in *True Grit* (1969), John Wayne had nothing more to prove. He was almost a guarantee at the box office, was beloved by audiences over thirty, and even managed to skirt blowback from his awkward politics in the 60s and his terrible film *The Green Berets* (1968), which was pro-Vietnam.

So, when this towering actor accepted a supporting role in *The Cowboys*, it seemed like an odd decision for him. Based on a novel by William Dale Jennings, the film is about a rancher, Wil Andersen (Wayne), who hires young boys as his cowhands when his team abandons him to join the gold rush. A group of men shows up on the ranch looking for work, but when Andersen catches the leader, Watts (Bruce Dern), in a lie, he sends them on their way. After a few days on his ranch teaching the boys the basics of herding, Andersen is confident they can learn the rest on the trail.

As they set out and drive the cattle, we see the men Andersen sent away surreptitiously shadowing them. It becomes clear they intend to ambush the boys and take the herd. Finally flushed out, face to face with Andersen, Watts is beaten senseless but retaliates when Andersen goes to leave. The bullets graze Andersen's arm and leg, but Watts takes two more shots that badly wound him. Watts and his men ride off with the herd, leaving the boys with Andersen, who dies by morning. Before he dies, he tells the boys he is proud of them.

Angry and ashamed for not standing up to the men, though they were following Andersen's orders, the boys get their guns out of the lock box on the chuck wagon and chase after Watts. They take on his gang and kill them all, ending Watts by dragging him behind a horse. They finish their job delivering the herd and buy a headstone inscribed with "Beloved Husband and Father." They place it near Andersen's burial spot.

This was not the first time Wayne had portrayed a father figure, but it would be the last, and he gave one of his finest performances. The fact that he died in the film was initially a massive shock to audiences and critics, but it did not remain a secret for long. Bruce Dern was reviled as Watts and knew going into the project he would instantly become the most hated man in America for shooting John Wayne.

Of course, Wayne and Dern are outstanding in the film, but so is Roscoe Lee Browne as the well-spoken cook. A Martinez and Robert Carradine were standouts among the boys, and the wonderful Colleen Dewhurst has a small part in the film.

Mark Rydell would go on to be among the most reliable directors of the decade, never an artist but a solid craftsman who never let the studio down. *The Cowboys* was a box office success, though some criticized the fact that the boys mature into men through violence and the use of guns. How many in the Old West did precisely that?

“This was not the first time Wayne had portrayed a father figure, but it would be the last, and he gave one of his finest performances.”

“One can almost smell the cedars and forest when they arrive in Minnesota. The cinematography is breathtaking.”

THE EMIGRANTS (1972)

DIRECTED BY Jan Troell
COUNTRY Sweden

One of the greatest films to emerge from Sweden, a country rich in film culture, *The Emigrants* was an immediate success with both audiences and critics. Set in 1844, the film explores the events surrounding a Swedish family's immigration to America, and their settling in Minnesota, overcoming often insurmountable odds.

When farming in Sweden proves too difficult, the land far too rocky and harsh, Karl (Max von Sydow), who assumed control of the farm after his father was injured moving a large rock, and his wife, Kristina (Liv Ullmann), decide to move to the United States. Initially unhappy about moving to America, Kristina challenges Karl, finally agreeing to go after her daughter Anna dies from food poisoning after eating uncooked porridge. With a group of other Swedes, they make the arduous journey by ship. Kristina is initially appalled that Ulrika (Monica Zetterlund), a well-known prostitute, travels with them. The two set aside their differences after one of Kristina's children is lost, and Ulrika finds the child and returns the babe to Kristina safe.

Arriving in New York, the Swedish are stunned at the sheer size of the city. They head for Minnesota but lose more of their group to illness. Though Kristina remains sanctimonious with her husband, she thaws and becomes best friends with Ulrika, coming to love the woman like a sister, which is mutual.

They arrive in Minnesota and realize the land is fertile, fantastically so, and Karl builds their home with the help of his friends. The film ends here and is picked up in the sequel *The New Land* (1973) filmed at the same time but released a year later.

Gritty and raw, with an almost documentary feel to it, the film beautifully captures what it must have been like to be entirely dependent on and at the mercy of the land for survival. One can almost smell the cedars and forest when they arrive in Minnesota. The cinematography is breathtaking. Ullmann and the great Max von Sydow are both superb, and there is a powerful supporting performance from Zetterlund as Ulrika. The actors bring great humanity to the characters, concurrently capturing their heartache and stoicism.

The Emigrants was an immediate success with audiences in Sweden and America and, to the surprise of many, was nominated for four Academy Awards, including Best Picture, Best Director, Best Actress (Ullmann), and Best Screenplay Adaptation. Ullmann won the Golden Globe for Best Actress (Drama) and Best Actress from the New York Film Critics circle. The same year *The Emigrants* was vying for Academy Awards, *The New Land* (1973) was a nominee for Best Foreign Language Film, the award *The Emigrants* won the year before.

It remains one of the finest films and sequels to come out of Sweden and established Troell as an international filmmaker.

Opposite Max von Sydow and Liv Ullmann as the struggling couple in search of a new home.

60

THE GODFATHER (1972)

DIRECTED BY Francis Ford Coppola
COUNTRY USA

Opposite A rare quiet moment between father and son.

"I believe in America" are the first words in Francis Ford Coppola's masterpiece *The Godfather*. Spoken by the undertaker Bonasera, he is an immigrant from Italy who came to America for a better way of life. Now, in 1945, he is at a wedding hosted by Don Vito Corleone (Marlon Brando), the most powerful Mafia leader in his beloved America. He is about to use an old Sicilian tradition, asking a favour of the bride's father on his daughter's wedding day. Bonasera wants justice the courts of America did not give him after his own daughter was viciously beaten and raped by a group of boys. He wants them dead. But Don Corleone will not do that because the young men did not kill the girl. "Make them suffer as she suffers," asks the old man.

Corleone admonishes the man, saying he was never a friend until now because he needs his help. Insulted that Bonasera offers to pay him, Corleone gets ready to terminate the meeting but instead acquiesces. In return, Corleone wants Bonasera's loyalty, friendship, and a promise to return the favour someday.

"Be my friend, Godfather," says Bonasera, kissing his hand.

Later in the film, standing over the bullet-riddled body of his eldest son, Sonny (James Caan), Corleone comes to Bonasera in the middle of the night to ask for his favour. Shaking, he stands over his beloved son and asks Bonasera to restore his son so the casket may be open. He then breaks down, crying, "See how they have massacred my boy!"

Coppola's *The Godfather* is about the Mafia and its inner workings, but it is also about a father and his sons, family, and loyalty. And *The Godfather* is about the American dream. Young Vito Corleone came to America with nothing and achieved wealth and power through hard work, smarts, and crime. He runs his crime family with an iron fist, training his sons, except Michael (Al Pacino) and adopted son Tom (Robert Duvall), to be a part of it. Sonny is a deadly executioner and hot-tempered killer for his father, while Fredo (John Cazale) is his father's bodyguard. Tom was treated like family, sent to law school, and then asked to work for Corleone. And Michael, the youngest, is a war hero, performing acts of bravery for strangers, as his father says, refusing to be a part of the business. Yet after the attempted assassination of his father, Michael volunteers to kill the men responsible. After that, Michael becomes the heir apparent to the Corleone empire, trains under his father to take over the business, and settles all scores after his father dies, executing the heads of the other Mafia families, making the Corleones the most powerful crime organization in America.

When Paramount was searching for a director for the film, they settled on Coppola, at that point an Oscar-winning writer (for *Patton* (1970), because he was Italian and because they felt they could control him. They learned very quickly that no one controls Coppola. Despite the misgivings of the company producing the film, he chose the cast, including box office poison Marlon Brando. The studio believed Brando's best work was long behind him. Upon reviewing early footage, however, they realized he was perfect for the role. But they felt it was too dark and were preparing to fire Coppola. Brando made it clear that if they fired Coppola, he would leave the project.

Coppola stayed and directed the film his way, creating, as one critic stated, "the greatest American film since *Citizen Kane*," which was high praise indeed. The film was an intimate study of the dichotomy of a vicious criminal and a loving family man. The violence was shocking, including a bloody horse's head, placed in the bed of a movie mogul as a warning. It was a first on so many levels.

An immediate critical and box office hit, *The Godfather* became an absolute phenomenon. Brando's name was revived, and the careers of Al Pacino, James Caan, Robert Duvall, Diane Keaton, and John Cazale were launched. Portraying a man in his seventies while he was just forty-five, Brando was breath-taking from his first moments on the screen. But the best

"The film has lost not a shred of its overwhelming power in the last fifty years."

performance in the film was Pacino, who we first see as a smiling young war hero in love. By the end of the picture, has evolved into a cold-hearted, ruthless killer, and it is an astounding character arc.

The film received ten Academy Award nominations, including Best Picture, Best Director, Best Actor (Brando), and three for Best Supporting Actor (Pacino, Caan, and Duvall). Coppola and Mario Puzo also received nominations for Best Screenplay Adaptation.

On Oscar night, the cast and crew watched *Cabaret* win award after award, including Best Director! But then Coppola won for the screenplay, Brando won (and refused) the Oscar for Best Actor, and *The Godfather* won Best Picture.

The film has lost not a shred of its overwhelming power in the last fifty years. It is as spellbinding today as it ever was and routinely tops lists as the greatest American film ever made.

"Both actors were suddenly on the radar of everyone casting in Hollywood."

THE KING OF MARVIN GARDENS (1972)

DIRECTED BY Bob Rafelson
COUNTRY USA

Jack Nicholson and Bruce Dern were both talents on the rise in the early 70s, two of the most exciting actors working in film. Dern had been in film longer, working in Roger Corman "B movies" for years, while Nicholson toiled as a writer, acting sporadically, waiting for that elusive big break. The two men were friends, and each held the other in high esteem, knowing their time would come.

The breaks came, Nicholson in *Easy Rider* (1969) earning an Oscar nomination for Best Supporting Actor, whereas Dern took the tougher route, playing a deranged cowboy who shoots John Wayne in the back and kills him partway through *The Cowboys* (1972). Both actors were suddenly on the radar of everyone casting in Hollywood, with Nicholson having the slight edge.

In *The King of Marvin Gardens*, they got their first chance to work together. They were both thrilled to be playing brothers and went into the project fully committed to director Bob Rafelson. Whatever he wanted from them, they gave him.

Things began rocky, but very quickly, everyone involved adapted. Originally, the actors were to play the other's part, but during a rehearsal, director Rafelson, doing an actors' exercise, asked them to switch roles. They did, and all three men liked the dynamic far more than they had the original casting. So, Dern became Jason, the brash, bold conman, and Nicholson became the meek, quiet radio DJ caring for his ailing grandfather.

The brothers meet in Atlantic City, where Jason has a get-rich scheme for which he needs his brother and his girlfriend, Sally (Ellen Burstyn), and the woman's daughter, Jessica (Julia Anne Robinson). The scheme falls through, and Jason announces that he plans to go away with Jessica leaving Sally behind. In a fit of rage, Sally shoots and kills Jason. Shocked but not surprised, David is left to escort his brother's body home to Philadelphia.

The film opens with a haunting monologue being read on the radio by David, which we are led to believe is the real thing, only to see it is not. Nothing is ever quite as it seems; that is the message.

Dern gives a big, bold performance as Jason, a born huckster who believes that lies are more interesting than the truth and that his fabricated life is far more exciting than reality. We know he is painfully aware of what he is. We catch it in his defeated eyes from time to time, but no one else seems to see it.

Nicholson is the quieter brother, more introspective, likely aware of his brother's lies and schemes but lacking the confidence to confront him. Having been shouted down too often throughout his life, he is used to going along with things.

The two women are superb, Burstyn the stronger. The shattered look of defeat on her face when her worst fears become a reality and Jason chooses her daughter over her. It sends her over the edge, willing to commit murder. Robinson is terrific as the daughter, a strong performance from this promising actress who died in an apartment fire just four years later.

The King of Marvin Gardens earned respectable reviews but did not do well at the box office. Audiences found the film a few years later with the advent of video rentals. Today it is appreciated for the performances of Dern and Nicholson, who each went off in a different direction after the film, remaining friends. This was the last genuinely outstanding film Bob Rafelson ever made.

Opposite For a change, Nicholson plays the quiet, conservative David to Dern's outrageous Jason.

"As sequels go, *The New Land* is excellent though does not surpass *The Emigrants.*"

THE NEW LAND (1972)

DIRECTED BY Jan Troell
COUNTRY Sweden

This movie begins where we left off with *The Emigrants* (1972). *The New Land* explores the hardships of the Swedes who have decided to build homes in Minnesota. Beyond the elements, the harsh winters, the constant hunt for food, and the attacks by the Indigenous peoples who are not happy about their arrival, the new immigrants must deal with debilitating illnesses, child mortality, life-threatening pregnancies, and extreme loneliness.

The New Land is every bit as authentic and realistic as *The Emigrants*, and Troell made the sound decision to start shooting the sequel right after the first film. This gave the overall look of the film a greater sense of continuity and allowed Troell artistic freedoms he might not have had if they had broken production and come back a year or more later. Creating the sequel on the heels of the first allowed consistency in the look of the characters and the sets and ensured the actors were available.

The narrative continues, following Karl and Kristina Oskar and their family members who have now settled in Minnesota. Things start to look brighter when Robert, Karl's brother, returns from his journey with a great deal of money. The banknotes turn out to be counterfeit. Another hit for Karl on top of the news is that Kristina has decided to have more children despite her doctor warning her it could be deadly. Working tirelessly to make a home, they are beset by troubles, including a massacre of more than thirty of their group. Kristina suffers through several miscarriages and finally dies in Karl's arms.

Karl lives to a ripe old age, swimming in the memories of his family and their journey to America. He dies an American citizen. By the time of his death, his children and grandchildren have forgotten they could ever speak Swedish.

Once again, Troell captures the rugged forests of Minnesota and shows the challenges faced by the families who migrated here in the mid-1800s. The narrative makes evident Karl's love for America; he tries to fight in the Civil War, but his damaged leg prevents it. For the most part, Kristina regrets the move, but her sanctimonious ways fade the longer she is away from her beloved homeland.

Max von Sydow shines in the second film, and Liv Ullmann is again terrific, but this time the film belongs to the lead actor.

As sequels go, *The New Land* is excellent though does not surpass *The Emigrants*. Like the first film, it received an Academy Award nomination for Best Foreign Language film.

Opposite Ullmann and von Sydow share one of the few happy scenes in this bleak film.

66 THE POSEIDON ADVENTURE (1972)

DIRECTED BY Ronald Neame
COUNTRY USA

Opposite The doomed passengers of the *Poseidon* navigate their way off the overturned ship.

Ronald Neame might have directed *The Poseidon Adventure*, but it was an Irwin Allen film. Allen was a hands-on producer who had a vision for all his productions. He always left his indelible mark.

Airport (1970) started the disaster film genre, but *The Poseidon Adventure*, based on the book by Paul Gallico, perfected the formula. A disaster film needed a group of people, a cross-section of society, all in one place, add a disaster of some kind that leaves them in absolute peril, employ a special-effects extravaganza, and then decide who comes out at the other end. The cast typically comprises veteran actors with a few big names. In this case, it was Gene Hackman as a take-charge minister.

When a massive tidal wave strikes the *Poseidon* cruise ship on New Year's Eve, it overturns, leaving the survivors to find their way back up to the top of the vessel. The narrative is as paint-by-numbers as you can get, but the execution is complex. This was not an easy film to make. Beyond the physical challenges, the actors also needed to connect with the audience to gain sympathy. Considering the script didn't give them much to work with, it was up to the actors to colour in the characters.

The fine performances carried *The Poseidon Adventure*, making it a great ride and a box office hit. Hackman led the way as the stern minister, with Ernest Borgnine and Stella Stevens as a trash-talking married couple. Jack Albertson and Shelley Winters are a long-time, happily married Jewish couple; Roddy McDowall is a crew member; Red Buttons is a shy, lonely man who has given up on love; and Pamela Sue Martin and Eric Shea are siblings travelling to see their parents in Greece.

They make their way through the treacherous, upside-down world. Not all of them will survive, though the one that hits the hardest is Winters's character. Now a grandmother, she was once a swimming champ and saves them when she dives into the water to find an opening. The stress brings about a heart attack, and she dies in the minister's arms on the other side.

"Please, not this woman," he weeps as she succumbs to her ravaged heart, leaving audiences heartbroken. Shelley Winters lost out for Best Actress despite her tremendous performance. She and Hackman stand out, but in fairness, the cast is a fine ensemble. Ernest Borgnine is all bluster as the tough cop who truly loves his sarcastic wife, nicely played by Stella Stevens; Red Buttons, by this point in his career, had the gentle, shy man down to an art form; Carol Lynley was fine as the terrified singer, and the two children were each equally annoying.

The minister sacrifices himself when he plunges to a fiery death after saving the others. As the formula prescribes, a group survives, but beloved cast members die.

The Poseidon Adventure was nominated for eight Academy Awards and would win two, one of them a Special Achievement Award for Visual Effects, the second for Best Song ("The Morning After," which became a hit on AM radio across North America). The movie was a massive success at the box office and received lukewarm reviews. But it did not matter what the film critics thought; audiences fell in love with it.

The disaster genre was here to stay.

“***Airport*** **started the disaster film genre, but *The Poseidon Adventure* perfected the formula.”**

68 AMERICAN GRAFITTI (1973)

DIRECTED BY George Lucas
COUNTRY USA

Opposite Ron Howard and Candy Clark enjoy a cold drink during the production of this surprising film.

If you first watched *American Graffiti* when you were under thirty years old, watch again, and you will find the film has grown in power and relevance. After seeing it later in life, I remember thinking, "I knew that kid. I was that kid!" George Lucas has never been a great director, despite his success with *Star Wars* (1977). But he knew this world in *American Graffiti* because he lived it as a teenager in Modesto, California. As a teenager, he and his friends spent endless nights in gleaming cars, cruising the streets and listening to rock and roll.

The setting is 1962, a year before the assassination of President John F. Kennedy, an event that would forever change the United States. Later, as Vietnam raged, the angry youth rebelled against the war, bringing about the counterculture movement. As Bob Dylan sang with conviction, "The times they are a-changin'."

Lucas explores the last Labor Day weekend in the lives of a group of teenagers blissfully unaware they are about to undergo life-altering change. The night is just beginning as they gather at Mel's Drive-In with the waitresses on roller skates. Steve (Ron Howard) and Curt (Richard Dreyfuss) plan to leave town the following day, flying off to college and a new life. The rest will stay behind: Laurie (Cindy Williams), Steve's girlfriend and Curt's little sister; Terry (Charles Martin Smith), the geek of the group; and John Milner (Paul Le Mat), the older tough guy of the group who cannot escape being a teenager. The night's events will impact two others new to the group: Carol (Mackenzie Phillips), who rides around with John most of the night, and Debbie (Candy Clark), a ditsy blonde who connects with Terry despite his plethora of lies throughout the night. It seems like a lifetime is lived in a few hours by these kids, and by morning, Steve is no longer leaving. He cannot be apart from Laurie.

As the plane carrying Curt climbs higher into the sky, we learn how the story ends for the main characters. Steve and Laurie will marry and divorce a few years later; Curt is a writer living in Canada, no doubt to escape the draft; Terry is MIA in Vietnam; and John is killed by a drunk driver, his greatest fear. After an entertaining few hours, Lucas leaves us sombre, contemplating life's unexpected turns. The cast were unaware of their characters' outcomes until they saw the film's premiere.

American Graffiti was a perfect fit for Lucas, and audiences responded, making the film a huge box office hit. The performances were exceptional, especially Candy Clark, Paul Le Mat, and Mackenzie Phillips. The songs on the soundtrack became best sellers again, and the film would usher in a nostalgia craze that spilled onto television. *Happy Days* and *Laverne and Shirley*, set in America's burnished past, became massive hits.

American Graffiti received six Oscar nominations, Best Picture and Best Director among them, with only Clark nominated among the actors. Sadly, nothing won. Yet it found something else, a timelessness that few films possess. As those gleaming cars cruise the streets, driven by young people, with rock and roll spilling out of the windows, we see a glimpse of the last year of innocence in America.

"After an entertaining few hours, Lucas leaves us sombre, contemplating life's unexpected turns."

"*Badlands* has maintained its brilliance. It's hard to understand why the film was a box office failure."

BADLANDS (1973)

DIRECTED BY Terrence Malick
COUNTRY USA

At the height of the French New Wave, director Jean-Luc Godard explained that all one needed for a film's narrative was "a guy, a girl, and a gun." *Badlands* is a perfect example.

It is a sparse film loosely based on the killing spree of Charles Starkweather in and around Lincoln, Nebraska, where Starkweather and a young girl massacred ten innocent people. An investigation proved Starkweather alone was guilty of the killings; the girl joined him without knowing his intentions. She thought he looked like James Dean, was smitten, and went along.

Watching the film today, we realize its influences on films like *True Romance* (1993), *Natural Born Killers* (1994), and *Kalifornia* (1993). Quentin Tarantino proudly announced his devotion to the film when he emerged as a promising new filmmaker in the early 90s. Many other new directors cited the film as an influence.

Malick made just two films in the 70s, yet each had a devoted following, and he remained relevant without making a new film for twenty years. When he announced he was making a war film, *The Thin Red Line* (1998), big-name actors dropped their rates to have a chance at working with the director.

Badlands has maintained its brilliance. It's hard to understand why the film was a box office failure, never finding its audience. Rediscovered when video cassette rentals became the rage in the early 80s, *Badlands* would become as revered as its director.

A pure combination of psychopath and sociopath, Kit cannot love, and it seems only a matter of time before he turns the gun on the young girl. Martin Sheen is electrifying as Kit, the deranged young man who enjoys killing. Like James Dean in *Giant* (1956), playing the young ranch hand Jett Rink, you cannot take your eyes off him. He is terrifying because of his lack of regard for his victims, pulling the trigger as easily as combing his hair. Sheen offers one of the most nuanced portrayals of psychosis captured on screen.

Spacek is excellent as Holly, a waif taken from her home after witnessing her father killed by Kit. She sees horrors no young person should endure. This movie put her on the path to an award-winning career.

Malick directed the film with a sure hand and absolute confidence, focusing on the two young outlaws. *Badlands* might be the most influential film of the 70s that few have heard of or seen.

Opposite Martin Sheen and Sissy Spacek launched their careers with this influential film.

72 ENTER THE DRAGON (1973)

DIRECTED BY Robert Clouse
COUNTRY China/USA

Opposite The diminutive but powerful Bruce Lee in his prime.

Bruce Lee.

The name renders the image of a martial arts god, and he might have been. His diminutive stature belied his strength, sculpted body, and ability to strike with flying fists and quick feet, and a fierce and furious intensity. His martial arts skills made him virtually indestructible by another human being, even when outnumbered five to one! He was lethal. By the time he became a major movie star in 1973, he had been working in the business for many years, beginning as a child actor and gaining fame co-starring as sidekick Kato on the popular *The Green Hornet* series.

Lee studied martial arts and created the Jeet Kune Do technique, based on unarmed combat techniques in which a fighter uses his hands, feet, and mind as weapons. Its popularity swept the world, but it was on screen that Lee gained his greatest fame.

In a series of martial arts films, Bruce Lee became an international superstar. Posters of Lee were in the bedrooms of young people around the globe, and long queues formed around the block to see his new releases.

Enter the Dragon was the first and generally considered the best of his movies. Was there ever a plot? Sort of, but it boiled down to Bruce Lee against the bad guys and little else. The films were widely interchangeable, with few differences other than the beautifully choreographed fight scenes, usually created by Lee himself.

Yet as fast as fame came, he was gone, dying on July 20, 1973, of a cerebral oedema at the age of thirty-two. For years, we heard whispers that a Chinese cartel murdered Lee, but those rumours have since been dispelled. Films he had made before his death were subsequently released, the most notable being *Return of the Dragon* (1974), where he and fellow martial arts star Chuck Norris fight in the Colosseum in Rome.

Gold Crest Film Studios made untold millions and firmly established themselves on the actor's name. His films set off a martial arts craze that saw Kung Fu studios popping up in every strip mall in North America for a time, as well as a hit TV series, *Kung Fu*, and even a pop song, "Kung Fu Fighting." Lee's influence still exists in the violent cage matches, which allow blends of Kung Fu and street fighting. Lee was recently a character in Quentin Tarantino's *Once Upon a Time in Hollywood* (2019), portrayed as the preening egomaniac he was said to be.

"Posters of Lee were in the bedrooms of young people around the globe."

74 **“Pauline Kael of *The New Yorker*, who could be a brutal critic, hailed the film as one of the greatest works of art ever created.”**

LAST TANGO IN PARIS (1973)

DIRECTED BY Bernardo Bertolucci
COUNTRY France/Italy

The storm of controversy that greeted the release of this film at the New York Film Festival in 1973 ended with a rave review from Pauline Kael of *The New Yorker*. Kael, who could be a brutal critic, hailed the film as one of the greatest works of art ever created. She gave the film instant credibility. The film marked a complete comeback for Marlon Brando, who would also soon win an Oscar for *The Godfather* (1972).

Working with Bernardo Bertolucci for the first time, a gifted new emerging filmmaker, Brando found a filmmaker who adored him and celebrated his need for improvisation. Bertolucci allowed Brando to improvise nearly the entire film, bringing elements of his own life to flesh out the character, Paul, an American adrift in Paris.

Paul is grieving the recent suicide of his wife, Rosa. He has also learned that she had a lover who was a complete copy of Paul, with the same robe, slippers, same everything. Rosa had orchestrated this, perhaps searching for the Paul she knew when they first met and fell in love before the melancholy set in.

The film is a long primal scream at life, grief, loss, regrets, sex, and pain. In the film's opening, we see Paul screaming at the top of his lungs as a train passes over, drowning his scream, silencing his anguish. He meets a twenty-two-year-old woman named Jeanne (Maria Schneider); they begin a torrid sexual relationship without exchanging personal information, not even their names. Despite their decision to keep it purely sexual, he begins to fall in love with her.

For three days, they meet. Paul tests her, humiliating her with sexual acts of degradation until he is convinced of her loyalty. But by then, it is too late. She has seen him for what he is and wants no part of a relationship with him. When he follows her home, she shoots him dead. When she reports it to the police as an attempted rape, she truthfully tells them, "I don't know his name."

In the nearly fifty years since its release, the landscape regarding such topics as consent has led to differing opinions of Bertolucci's treatment of the material, particularly the rape scene. Many years after its release, Schneider had reported feeling mistreated and abused by her director and co-actor. But at the time, most of the talk was regarding the graphic scenes and erotic drama, which was entirely new for audiences.

Brando's performance was absolute genius, drawing on his own past to fill in the blanks on Paul's life It is an astounding piece of acting, notably the scene with his dead wife, lying beside her in her bed, raging at her for leaving him. Filled with anguish, he tells her he wishes he had the courage to do what she has done. It is a brilliant, unsettling scene by an actor at the peak of his considerable talent and shot by a filmmaker with absolute trust in his leading man.

Schneider was commended for her courage in performing such explicit scenes with sex and nudity and for her trust in Bertolucci and Brando, but her performance never compares with Brando.

The film was X-rated in the United States when first released but looks tame today. Still, it's a ground-breaking work that earned Brando and Bertolucci both Academy Award nominations for Best Actor and Best Director. Though Brando deserved to win, there was no chance of another Oscar after he refused the award for *The Godfather* the year before.

Opposite Marlon Brando and Maria Schneider make an odd yet compelling couple.

"Bogdanovich gave audiences a beautiful film, perfectly capturing the barren land of the Midwest, the sad, lonely towns."

PAPER MOON (1973)

DIRECTED BY Peter Bogdanovich
COUNTRY USA

On the strength of two films, *The Last Picture Show* (1971) and the screwball comedy *What's Up Doc?* (1972), Peter Bogdanovich was among the new young toasts of Hollywood, and he knew it. Bogdanovich had already left his wife, although he retained her as a creative partner, and had taken up with the starlet Cybill Shepherd, whom he believed to be a major talent. Insiders at the time disapproved, and the couple quickly became alienated.

Bogdanovich made a third great film in the 70s, again paying homage to the films of years gone by with *Paper Moon*, adapted from the novel *Addie Pray*. Bogdanovich loved the period-piece story and approached Ryan O'Neal to play the lead role of Moses, a conman on the road in 1936. For the crucial role of his ten-year-old partner, Addie, his ex-wife Polly Platt convinced him to look at Tatum O'Neal, Ryan's daughter. He did, and she was cast.

The film was shot in black and white, giving it the look of the road comedies of the 30s, and though often very funny, the film is loaded with sadness as well, as the Depression is in full swing, and the people of America are hurting. Moses encounters Addie at her mother's funeral, where it is suspected he might be her father. He agrees to deliver Addie to her aunt but first visits the man who killed her mother with his car and collects $200 from him. Overhearing the conversation, Addie demands her share very loudly in a restaurant, and Moses, busted, agrees. But he doesn't have it because he spent most of the money fixing up his broken-down Model T. They hit the road selling Bibles to grieving widows, conning them into thinking their recently departed husbands bought the Bibles for them before they died. Addie gets in on the scam and proves as good as Moses at conning people.

After picking up the floozy Trixie Delight (Madeline Kahn) and her maid, Addie becomes jealous and engineers a way for Moses to catch Trixie having sex with another man. He throws Trixie out; Addie gives the maid enough money to get home; and the two continue on their way, pulling cons from town to town.

Even after finally getting to her aunt's, Addie has no interest in being there and chases Moses down the road, reminding him he still owes her money. The car starts to roll away, and they end up jumping into the moving vehicle, together again.

The film earned strong reviews from North American critics who praised the lead performances and the work of Madeline Kahn. Audiences too flocked to the film, and *Paper Moon* was a solid box office hit. Nominated for four Academy Awards, it would win one, for Tatum O'Neal as Best Supporting Actress. Though worthy of the win, O'Neal was considered the lead in the film, and many felt she was in the wrong category. She became the youngest person to win an Oscar for acting.

Once again utilizing black and white, as he had in *The Last Picture Show*, Bogdanovich gave audiences a beautiful film, perfectly capturing the barren land of the Midwest, the sad, lonely towns, and the faces of the struggling people of the time.

Both O'Neals eventually faltered in the movie business, and though they still work sporadically, box office hits were many years ago. It was also the last major hit for Bogdanovich for many years, and his personal life was in a shambles. He did come back briefly with *Mask* (1985) before returning to writing about film and becoming a noted historian.

Opposite Tatum and Ryan O'Neal with their director Peter Bogdanovich.

78 SERPICO (1973)

DIRECTED BY Sidney Lumet
COUNTRY USA

Opposite As an idealistic young police officer, Serpico (Al Pacino) placed his life in peril lashing back and fighting corruption within the department.

Frank Serpico always wanted to be a cop. He graduated and immediately joined the New York City Police Department. He quickly begins seeing corruption in the department as cops take bribes, falsify reports, and routinely beat the accused and witnesses. Many get rich from their stolen goods from crime sites, bribes, and pay-offs.

An honest cop with integrity, Serpico (Al Pacino) wants none of that; he is clean and would continue to be. He transfers units three times before the corruption is so widespread that he chooses to report it to his superiors. His fellow cops advise him to take the money and keep his mouth shut, saying he doesn't want to be a snitch among his peers and that he is asking for trouble. Serpico ignores them. Soon after his report, widespread investigations begin, and the other cops blame Serpico. He realizes the other cops no longer have his back when, during a chase, his partner refuses to come to his aid, and Serpico gets shot in the face.

Sweeping changes come through the New York Police Department as many cops are fired or charged with crimes. Although Serpico is branded a traitor within the police department, he is a hero in the newspapers. He decides to leave the United States and live in Switzerland, doing interviews when requests come in.

Pacino's honest, gritty performance in *Serpico* drew immediate acclaim and brought audiences into the cinema. After *The Godfather* (1972) and *Scarecrow* (1973), he was suddenly the hottest new young actor, and audiences wanted more. He captured Serpico's decency without coming off as preachy or self-righteous. Instead, he is a decent, honest cop dedicated to the oath he swore to serve and protect. Pacino beautifully captures the growing heartbreak he feels seeing the degree and depth of corruption, reaching the highest ranks.

Sidney Lumet gave the film enough authenticity to tell the story in the documentary style of *The French Connection* (1971).

Pacino was nominated for an Academy Award for his performance and won the Golden Globe for Best Actor (Drama) but lost the Oscar to Jack Lemmon in a sentimental vote from the Academy.

Serpico furthered the rise of Pacino, who followed this with his finest performance in *The Godfather Part II* (1974) and his electrifying work in *Dog Day Afternoon* (1975). *Serpico* marked the first of three consecutive Academy Award nominations for Best Actor.

“Pacino was suddenly the hottest new young actor, and audiences wanted more.”

80 THE EXORCIST (1973)

DIRECTED BY William Friedkin
COUNTRY USA

Opposite Max von Sydow and Jason Miller as two priests attempting to exorcise the demons from the levitating child played by Linda Blair.

Psycho (1960), Alfred Hitchcock's terrifying film, revolutionized the horror genre by having a man as the source of terror instead of a monster. No vampires, werewolves, or long-dead Egyptian mummy lumbering in chase of his victims. The beast in *Psycho* is a nice-looking young man who happens to be a murderer with a severe mother fixation. Norman Bates is utterly insane, butchering a young woman in the shower at the motel he operates. Oh, and he dresses up like his mother, who is stuffed in the house that looms over the motel.

About the same time as its release, we began to hear about a new type of killer in our midst, "the serial killer." Suddenly, the plot of *Psycho* became very real.

The Exorcist was based on a best-selling novel by William Peter Blatty, who wrote the screenplay for the film, and produced the picture for Warner Brothers. Allegedly, Blatty attended an actual exorcism with approval from the Catholic Church. The fact that Catholics had a creed within their beliefs called the Rite of Exorcism was enough to terrify the masses when they queued around city blocks to see the new film.

Ask anyone who saw the movie in a cinema, and they will tell you they walked out utterly terrified, forever altered by the sight of Linda Blair as the twelve-year-old girl possessed by the devil and the extraordinary events that take place in her room as two priests attempt to drive the devil out of her. One of them, Father Merrin (Max von Sydow), has performed many exorcisms, while the other, Father Karras (Jason Miller), is struggling with his faith and the recent death of his mother. Regan (Blair), the young girl, has seen every doctor in New York. Her mother, Chris (Ellen Burstyn), is a famous actress who wants her daughter cured, and she would like to keep it out of the media as well.

Early in the movie, we see Regan and her mother at the doctors' appointments, see the child throw her mother across a room, grab a doctor by the testicles and reduce him to a screaming child, and watch the girl viciously masturbate with a crucifix. However, nothing prepares us for that first time Karras goes through the door into the cold room where Regan/devil is. Restrained for her safety, she greets him with, "Your mother sucks cocks in hell, you worthless motherfucker." Her face no longer resembles that of a young girl; she is hideous, with scars and pus dripping from the wounds she has inflicted on her body. Her voice is guttural and deep. She can send vomit across the room at will and levitate, but she cannot get out of the restraints. A devil has indeed taken hold of this child.

The priests follow the prescribed method for exorcism. Eventually, Karras releases Regan by taking on the devil himself, leaping through a window, and falling to an agonizing death far below, killing both the creature and himself. It is an astounding study of faith as we watch tortured Karras find his again at the cost of his life and, in doing so, saves the child.

The cast is sublime, beginning with Jason Miller's tormented Father Karras, racked with guilt, and trying to do the right thing. Burstyn is outstanding as Chris; Blair superb as Regan, though her demonic voice came from character actress Mercedes McCambridge (who initially received no credit). Max von Sydow gave a towering performance as Father Merrin, a beautiful portrait of faith and dignity.

There is little doubt the Catholic Church and its belief in exorcism and the devil helped the film at the box office, giving it a grounding many horror films do not have.

Friedkin's powerful direction managed to fill us with terror and dread, breathlessly anticipating the unspeakable horrors that awaited us on the other side of that bedroom door. Though tame compared to some of the slasher horror films that came later, *The Exorcist* remains a work of art and continues to hold up.

"Ask anyone who saw the movie in a cinema, and they will tell you they walked out utterly terrified."

"With his performance in the film, Nicholson became the most popular actor of his time and arguably the most gifted."

THE LAST DETAIL (1973)

DIRECTED BY Hal Ashby
COUNTRY USA

In Hal Ashby's superb film, two Navy lifers escort a naive young sailor to the brig for stealing a donation box. Jack Nicholson was cast as Billy "Badass" Buddusky, who sees the trip as a chance to cut loose and do some hellraising. Mulhall (Otis Young), called "Mule," will accompany Buddusky on the journey, also happy to enjoy some recreation along the way. However, that all changes when they meet the shy young man they are taking to prison, Meadows, beautifully portrayed by Randy Quaid as a gentle giant who has experienced little of life.

Buddusky's conscience will not allow him to take this kid to prison for eight years without showing him a good time, knowing it will be his only chance. The boy is the kind of shy kid who will not return a hamburger even if it is undercooked. Buddusky, on the other hand, lives to make waves and be contrarian. He realizes they have Military Police (MPs) privileges while fulfilling this duty and can get away with pretty much anything. And so, he tries.

They discover very quickly that Meadows is a kleptomaniac. Despite this, they begin to take a shine to their prisoner. The men take him drinking, even though he is underage, strong-arming the bartender to serve him. Next stop is a whorehouse, where Meadows is matched with a kind-hearted young woman, portrayed by Carol Kane. The young man leaves believing she has feelings for him. Their craziest stop is a religious cult, where Badass, hoping to get some action, sees a strange sight when the people around him begin speaking in tongues. The look on his face is utterly priceless. And, of course, he starts a brawl when the opportunity presents itself.

To prove his manhood to his fearless new friends, Meadows attempts an escape. The two MPs catch Meadows and beat him to secure him, taking him to prison bruised and battered. And yet the good-natured young man does not have any hate for the guards. He still considers them his friends.

Before *The Last Detail* (1973) opened in North America, Nicholson had won the Best Actor prize at the Cannes Film Festival, leaving him deeply disappointed when he lost the Oscar to Jack Lemmon in *Save the Tiger*. Most thought it was a sentimental nod to Lemmon, more for a life's achievement than the actual performance.

With his performance in the film, Nicholson became the most popular actor of his time and arguably the most gifted. He could switch from smiling to rage in a heartbeat, and his explosions of anger were both funny and darkly frightening.

Randy Quaid was also nominated for Best Supporting Actor, as was Robert Towne for his profane screenplay. Both Otis Young and the luminous Carol Kane contributed fine performances to the film, gently guided by Ashby, who famously paid special attention to his actors on set. He captures the irony of what the men are doing, the sadness within all three, and yet the joys at the small bits of adventure they have along the way.

Five Easy Pieces (1970) and *Carnal Knowledge* (1971) had announced Nicholson's arrival as a major new actor; *The Last Detail* announced him as a star. He has walked that fine line as actor and star ever since.

Opposite Jack Nicholson, Otis Young, and Randy Quaid on their train journey just before they get diverted.

"Beautifully mounted and superbly directed by Sydney Pollack, it remains one of the most iconic works of the 70s."

THE WAY WE WERE (1973)

DIRECTED BY Sydney Pollack
COUNTRY USA

For a romantic movie to work, it requires chemistry between the two lovers. If the audience does not believe the two characters love each other, the film's entire premise fails. But it's usually a guaranteed win when it works, like Scarlett and Rhett in *Gone with the Wind* (1939) and Rick and Ilsa in *Casablanca* (1942).

Such was the case with Katie and Hubbell in *The Way We Were* (1973).

Sydney Pollack's film was an instant hit with its sweeping score, the warm nostalgia, and the two lead performances by Robert Redford and Barbra Streisand. Both at the height of their popularity, they found an easy, relaxed connection with one another that transferred to the screen.

Katie is a college revolutionary, a fast-talking Jewish girl secretly in love with the all-American jock Hubbell who is a gifted writer. His writing causes her to fall deeper for him, but she never acts on it, thinking he would not have any interest. Years later, after the war, she encounters him in a bar, and they spend the night together. They become a couple, and Hubbell writes a novel that enjoys much acclaim and success. They journey to Hollywood to work on a movie adaptation. As Hubbell works within affluent Hollywood circles, McCarthyism is rearing its ugly head. Katie rages at him for selling out, squandering his gifts, and always taking the easiest route. She realizes that Hubbell is not the man she thought he was, and he tires of her polarizing and imposing outbursts. Eventually, despite having a daughter together, they part.

Years later, after their divorce, they encounter one another on the streets of New York City. They exchange few words, but the longing is still there. He is now writing for TV, the ultimate sell-out, and she is organizing anti-war demonstrations. Though worlds apart politically, even morally, there is undeniable love between them. She brushes his hair aside one last time and then returns to her work. It is one of the most heartbreaking endings.

The performances are perfect. Both received Oscar nominations that year, although Redford's was for his work in *The Sting*. Most agree this was the finer performance. He is superb as that flawed American Adonis who cannot see in him what others can and fears reaching for the heavens. Audiences adored the couple in the film, making the film one of the year's biggest box office hits.

The title song won an Oscar for composer Marvin Hamlisch, setting him on a successful career.

The years have been kind to *The Way We Were*. Although there has been talk of a sequel, ego always got in the way. At one point, Streisand insisted on directing, but by then, Redford was an Oscar-winning director and had his own interest in helming the picture. The film never got its sequel. Just as well, it gives the original film greater power. Beautifully mounted and superbly directed by Sydney Pollack, it remains one of the most iconic works of the 70s.

Opposite Barbra Streisand looking ready to unload at a party with the unsuspecting Robert Redford.

86 CHINATOWN (1974)

DIRECTED BY Roman Polanski
COUNTRY USA

Opposite Nicholson and his outrageous bandage alongside the exquisite Faye Dunaway.

John Huston established many parameters for the genre "film noir" with his superb film *The Maltese Falcon* (1941). The movies, set in the world of crime and its underbelly, were acting showcases for the likes of Humphrey Bogart and James Cagney. The genre remains popular today with films such as *The Usual Suspects* (1995) and the magnificent *L.A. Confidential* (1997). Many critics and historians choose *Chinatown* as the greatest in the film noir genre, me included.

Chinatown was perfectly cast. The dense, twisting screenplay, written by Robert Towne, offered three central roles for powerful actors. Jack Nicholson is J. J. Gittes, the private investigator; Faye Dunaway is the femme fatale/victim Evelyn Mulwray; and the great film director John Huston is Noah Cross, the demonic father of Mulwray. It was a dream cast for director Roman Polanski. It's a dark, bleak plot, with Huston portraying the most despicable of villains and an ending no one saw coming.

The film is beautiful to behold with outstanding period production design and exquisite costumes of the era. It is a flawless recreation of the 1930s. To the credit of the actors, none of them look out of place in a period thriller.

Jack Nicholson, by this time, was a superstar who happened to be an enormously gifted actor, beloved by both audiences and critics. He is cast here as a Bogart-esque private eye in California before the war. He gives one of his finest performances as the hot shot who gets blindsided by the case. Gittes never thought life could be as twisted and corrupt as things are in the Cross-Mulwray family. Even though he has experience with the dark underbelly in Chinatown, Gittes does not expect what happens here.

When Gittes, tired of being played for a fool, slaps Evelyn and demands to know who the mysterious young girl is, she answers, "She's my sister [slap], she's my daughter [slap] my sister... she's my daughter AND my sister," and at last Gittes knows the terrible truth. Cross raped his daughter and has covered it up all these years but now wants to get his hands on the child he conceived with his daughter. Evelyn will go to the ends of the earth to prevent this, and Gittes knows it. As Evelyn tries to escape with her daughter, the police shoot at her, hitting her in the head. We see her eye explode out of her head, and so does her terrified daughter. Vile old Cross gathers the screaming girl in his arms and walks away with her, while a cop tells Gittes, "Forget it Jake ... it's Chinatown," pulling the horrified Gittes away.

It received eleven Academy Award nominations, but it had little chance against *The Godfather Part II*. Only Robert Towne won that night for his superb screenplay. For his superbly horrifying Noah Cross, John Huston was passed over entirely.

Nicholson and Dunaway were superb in the lead roles, with crackling chemistry. Nicholson had the courage as an actor to go through most of the film with a heavy bandage on his nose from an earlier on-the-job incident. Dunaway's Evelyn, so damaged and broken, was the finest performance of her career though she would win her Oscar in *Network* (1976) two years later.

Chinatown would be the last film Roman Polanski would make on American soil. Found guilty of having sex with a minor, he fled the United States before sentencing and has remained a fugitive all these years, making some excellent films in Europe. When he won his Oscar for Best Director eighteen years later for *The Pianist* (2002), it was a complete surprise. Many believe *Chinatown* is his masterpiece and stands at the top of the greatest film noirs ever created.

"Many critics and historians choose *Chinatown* as the greatest in the film noir genre, me included."

LENNY (1974)

DIRECTED BY Bob Fosse
COUNTRY USA

Opposite Dustin Hoffman managed to capture the complex Lenny Bruce.

Bob Fosse's film biography of Lenny Bruce was a harsh look at a man who made comedy from headlines and rarely held back, using vulgar language, obscenities, and unbridled commentary about sex. Bruce was the godfather of comedy to people like Richard Pryor, George Carlin, Sarah Silverman, Robin Williams, and many others who stood in front of an audience with a microphone.

To portray Bruce, the director chose Dustin Hoffman, a hardcore Method actor who began listening to the recordings of Bruce, watching old 16mm films of his shows, and finding his way into the mind of this complicated man. The challenge was this: many comedians have proven themselves to be great actors, but can an actor portray a comic? Can they find the rhythm of the language of the comedian? Can they hit the punch lines? Could Dustin Hoffman play Bruce and be as funny?

The answer was a resounding yes.

In this harsh black and white film, Dustin Hoffman is brilliant as Lenny Bruce, a man who was as shocked as anyone that people would pay him to spout his opinions. Hoffman captured the fearlessness in Bruce's act, coming onstage, scanning the audience, finding visible minorities, and then calling them names. For his choice of words, he was dubbed a "sick comic" and banned from doing his act in many cities. But he used such hateful terms as "nigger" or "kike" to make a point. They were just words; they meant nothing. The tone and manner that accompanied the words were what needed to be considered. So, angered by the constant trips to jail and court, he began reading his courtroom transcripts to restless audiences who came to see him rant.

Heroin addiction eventually killed Bruce when he overdosed in his bathroom. His marriage to the famous stripper Honey Harlow (Valerie Perrine) was long over, and that relationship's toxicity warped them both. Each spent time in and out of drug rehab and mental institutions, each enabling the other.

Like all of Fosse's films, *Lenny* explores the personal cost of celebrity. Bruce begins a long downward slide almost at once upon becoming famous. Hoffman gives a riveting performance as the comic, capturing his rage but also his vulnerability and sadness. Perrine is excellent as Harlow, a woman who loved her husband but never really liked him.

The film received six Academy Awards nominations, including Best Picture, Best Actor, Best Actress, and Best Director. But since Fosse's *Cabaret* (1972) had swept the awards two years earlier, *Lenny* came home empty-handed.

Lenny was among the first biographies to explore its subject warts and all and was brilliant for it. A provocative and thoughtful study of a man who suffered the darkest side of show biz.

"The challenge was this: many comedians have proven themselves to be great actors, but can an actor portray a comic?"

"The film offers excellent performances, each is campy and in the spirit of the film in every way."

PHANTOM OF THE PARADISE (1974)

DIRECTED BY Brian De Palma
COUNTRY USA

Brian De Palma's rock and roll fable comes from the classic story *The Phantom of the Opera*. He had several versions for inspiration, including the 1925 production with Lon Chaney, 1943 with Claude Rains, and the Hammer version in 1962 with Herbert Lom. Not one of them is as much fun as De Palma's satirical horror film, which is more of a black comedy musical. The film became a cult classic, popular on midnight circuits, and often ran on a double bill with *The Rocky Horror Picture Show* (1975).

The years have been kind to the film, and today it remains one of the director's best, no small achievement considering he also created *Blow Out* (1981), *Scarface* (1983), and *Casualties of War* (1989).

Phantom of the Paradise is a playful, sometimes silly, often frightening romp through the horror genre, gently using the conventions of horror to make the film work.

Winslow Leach (William Finley) is a tall, gawky, and awkward composer who wants to get his work produced by Swan, a record producer who turns everything he touches to gold. Swan is looking for a ringer to open his new venue, "The Paradise." He hears Winslow playing his opera about Faust and knows his search is over. But Winslow wants to control the work, and Swan does not play well with anyone else—he wants the music, not the composer. He steals the music and has Winslow sent to prison. Winslow escapes and breaks into The Paradise to retrieve his music but is horribly disfigured and maimed by a record press. He dons a black cape and bird-like biker helmet and begins his new career haunting The Paradise.

Meanwhile, Swan has found his singer for the opera, a lovely girl named Phoenix (Jessica Harper), who had earlier befriended Winslow. She sings the work like she was born for it. Cutting a deal with the Phantom, which he intends to break, Swan gives him a degree of control over his work, provided the accidents stop. Swan even promises to restore the man's voice. When Winslow discovers that Swan has no intention of fulfilling his end of the bargain and that he has made a deal with the devil to make him immortal, he schemes to destroy Swan.

The film offers excellent performances, including Harper as Phoenix, diminutive Paul Williams as Swan, Finley as the Phantom, and Gerrit Graham as Beef, the swishy rock star. Each is campy and in the spirit of the film in every way.

And let's not forget the music, opening with the exciting "Goodbye Eddie," the Beach Boys-esque tune in which the Phantom makes his first appearance, and "Old Souls," a haunting song about forever love that speaks to the very soul of the film. The song score is superb despite not getting much attention over the years.

It would be unfair to credit *The Phantom of the Opera* as the only source material for the film, as Faust and Oscar Wilde's "The Picture of Dorian Gray" were clear inspirations. The film would launch the career of Brian De Palma. It received a single Academy Award for Best Song Score and Adaptation (no longer given). Actress Sissy Spacek served as a set decorator on the film and later starred in De Palma's *Carrie* (1976).

Opposite In this wild ride of a film, songwriter Paul Williams wrote the fantastic score and portrayed the immortal Swan who steals from the Phantom and pays the terrible price.

92 SWEPT AWAY (1974)

DIRECTED BY Lina Wertmüller
COUNTRY Italy

Opposite Giancarlo Giannini and Mariangela Melato arrive at their secluded island.

Lina Wertmüller was the most recognized female director in the world between 1972 and 1976 and became the first woman ever to be nominated for an Academy Award for Best Director for her masterpiece *Seven Beauties* (1975). Surprisingly, *Swept Away* garnered no awards.

This brilliant but troubling film was a demanding work to watch, filled with moments of misogyny, brutal violence towards women, and dismissal of the lower class. Like most Wertmüller films, this one explores class warfare in Italy. The wealthy believe they are an elevated class above the poor and treat them accordingly. Aboard a luxurious yacht in the pristine sea off the shores of Italy, a vacationing group of the privileged enjoy sunbathing, swimming, and drinking. One of the women, Raffaella (Mariangela Melato), takes great joy in targeting one of the workers aboard the ship with vicious verbal attacks. Gennarino (Giancarlo Giannini) does not respond, wanting to keep his job. Rafaella asks to go on a sunset tour in a small dinghy one evening, and he is assigned to accompany her.

The two become lost and end up stranded on an island with no food or water, just one another. Suddenly, the roles shift. She must rely on him to survive. He revels in his new power.

His treatment of her is difficult to watch. He beats her when she does anything that displeases him, yet something in their relationship is evolving. Having never been subservient to a man, never depended on a man for survival and protection, she becomes fascinated with him. Much to her surprise, she finds herself attracted to him, and they enjoy passionate sex on the beach throughout the days. She is content for the first time in her life. Stripped of her status and possessions, she is at ease and satisfied with this man. When a ship passes within range of the island, she does not signal it because she does not wish to return to civilization and her old life. He wants to test his island lover by seeing what she will do when they return. He signals the next ship that passes. He does not like the answer he gets. She flies away with her husband, never to see him again.

The actors superbly create authentic, intense characters, fearlessly showing their strengths and faults. Aboard the yacht, Raffaela is a nasty, entitled woman. On the island, she slowly evolves into a trusting, reliant woman, gradually and entirely changing her view of this man. Melato manages to make us believe both roles. Giannini is equally brilliant as a man who is a contradiction in terms. He abuses her, no question, lashing out with vicious slaps, but is convincing in showing us he has fallen in love with her. The two characters must demonstrate a near primal love, a lust born out of need, and Wertmüller and her fine actors beautifully create it.

The film received some positive reviews, though many took issue with the violence towards Raffaela. A forgettable remake with Madonna came out in 2002.

"The actors superbly create authentic, intense characters, fearlessly showing their strengths and faults."

"The absolute brilliance of Dreyfuss landed the film great reviews and talk of an Oscar nomination for the young star."

THE APPRENTICESHIP OF DUDDY KRAVITZ (1974)

DIRECTED BY Ted Kotcheff
COUNTRY Canada

Mordecai Richler's beloved and brilliant novel came to the screen in 1974 in a superb adaptation. Canadian filmmaker Ted Kotcheff made the film with loving care, with Richler himself writing the screenplay. The final ingredient was the decision to cast rising American actor Richard Dreyfuss as Duddy, a hyperactive hustler obsessed with making something of himself from his humble beginnings. He dedicates himself to making money, owning land, and earning the respect of others.

"A man without land is nothing," his wise old grandfather tells him, and Duddy hangs on every word his *zeyde* tells him. He begins his quest to be a landowner. While striving to purchase a property for a future resort, he betrays, lies, steals, bribes, cheats, and swindles, even with his best friends. Somehow, Dreyfuss offers a Duddy that wins our hearts; despite his deplorable actions, we cheer for him.

Perhaps it is because the film, like the book, explores how the odds were stacked against Duddy. He grew up in poverty, without a mother, a father who devotes his time and energy to his brother, a medical student. Duddy strives to earn the love of his family. He dreams of one day bequeathing a home on his resort to his father and his *zeyde*. But when the old man discovers how Duddy got the money to buy the land, he wants nothing to do with it or his grandson. Seeing Duddy finally for what he is, the grandfather shuns the boy. Meanwhile, his father and uncle cannot figure out what they had missed in their young prodigy.

Despite his disappointment, Duddy is buoyed when he is given a tab at the local diner—finally a somebody. He tries to forget that his actions led to a tragic accident, paralyzing his best friend, and costing him his girlfriend, the one person who could keep him grounded. When the local mob boss wants to do business with him, Duddy runs him off his property. He has some limits.

As expected, the film was a solid hit in Canada, where the novel was well known, but also in the United States, to the surprise of most. The absolute brilliance of Dreyfuss landed the film great reviews and talk of an Oscar nomination for the young star. He and fellow American Jack Warden, as his father, gave superb performances.

Dreyfuss creates the Duddy described in the novel to perfection. He is a grinning, demonic young man who worships the almighty dollar. His blazing eyes dance at the thought of a scam, tackling anyone who stands in his way. Always in motion, it is somewhat shocking when we see him sitting still. Though he proves to be something more than his uncle thought of him, he is, in fact, precisely the cheating "boy on the make" his uncle calls him.

Richler's screenplay is perfection and earned him an Oscar nomination, but sadly Dreyfuss was not nominated for Best Actor. He would win an Oscar for Best Actor in 1977 for *The Goodbye Girl*, but his work in *The Apprenticeship of Duddy Kravitz* was far superior. It is still widely considered among the best Canadian films ever made and one of the finest performances of Dreyfuss's career.

Opposite Richard Dreyfuss as Duddy alongside his father played by Jack Warden.

INTERMISSION: OUTSIDE THE MOVIE BRAT CIRCLE

Right Kubrick sets a scene for *Barry Lyndon* while Ryan O'Neal looks on.

Coppola, De Palma, Lucas, Scorsese, and Spielberg made up the movie brats of the 70s, also known as the geniuses behind the New American Cinema.

But let's remember the many other filmmakers, not household names, who created some of the decade's greatest films. They are lesser known to be sure, but every bit as gifted, hard-working, and dedicated to cinema as were the giants of the decade.

We'll start with Woody Allen, a one-time stand-up comic, and the great Stanley Kubrick. Allen had burst through with his early comedies *Bananas* (1971) and *Love and Death* (1975), but it was *Annie Hall* (1977) that made his name as a leading American director. He redefined the romantic comedy, adding a fourth component to the tried and true "boy meets girl, boy loses girl, boy gets girl back" with "boy loses girl forever." He ended the decade with his masterpiece *Manhattan* (1979), which was really a loving tribute to New York City.

Kubrick had been in film for many years, creating such masterpieces as *Paths of Glory* (1957), *Spartacus* (1960), his brilliant black comedy *Dr. Strangelove* (1964), and *2001: A Space Odyssey* (1968). He directed only two films in the 70s, both bold and visionary: *A Clockwork Orange* (1971), a disturbing piece about a dystopian society, which today, more than fifty years later, still looks futuristic, and *Barry Lyndon* (1975), his immersive story set in the 1700s, a stunning visual masterwork that has grown in stature through the years. Today, many consider *Barry Lyndon* his finest film.

Also among the filmmakers of the New American Cinema were two prolific men who shared the same name. Sidney Lumet, an actor's director, gave us *Serpico* (1973), *Dog Day Afternoon* (1975), *Network* (1976), and before that, *12 Angry Men* (1957), *Long Day's Journey into Night* (1962), and many others. Sydney Pollack was a mainstream favourite, directing *Jeremiah Johnson* (1972) and *The Way We Were* (1973), though his masterpiece remains *They Shoot Horses, Don't They?* (1969).

Former producer (*To Kill a Mockingbird*) Alan J. Pakula began directing in the late 60s but came into his own in the 70s with the superb thriller *Klute* (1971), *The Parallax View* (1974), the masterful *All the President's Men* (1976), and later *Starting Over* (1979). He seemed to possess an affinity for women, guiding Jane Fonda and later Meryl Streep to some of their finest achievements.

With his long hair, T-shirts, sandals, and ubiquitous joint, Hal Ashby was everything the studio system loathed, yet far too gifted to be ignored. An Oscar-winning film editor for *In the Heat of the Night* (1967), he began directing in the 70s and had an extraordinary ten-year run. Among his films were *The Landlord* (1970),

Harold and Maude (1972), a unique love story, *The Last Detail* (1973), which locked in Jack Nicholson as a major superstar, *Shampoo* (1975), *Bound for Glory* (1976), and his seething drama *Coming Home* (1978), one of the finest films about the conflict in Vietnam and its impact on the men coming back. He closed out the decade with the brilliant political satire *Being There* (1979).

Mel Brooks created a new form of comedy to suit his talents, the parody film, which spoofed classic genres of cinema. The first, *Blazing Saddles* (1974), blew apart the western genre with ribald jokes and wild sight gags that delighted audiences. Brooks was just warming up. The second, *Young Frankenstein* (1974), remains a comedic masterpiece, the best parody ever made, capping Brooks's career. *Silent Movie* (1976) had its moments, and *High Anxiety* (1977) spoofed Hitchcock and film noirs, but you needed to know the director and the genre for full appreciation.

Robert Altman had been busy in film and television but burst through with *M*A*S*H* (1970), a superb war comedy set in Korea but about Vietnam. He followed through the decade with acclaimed films such as *McCabe & Mrs. Miller* (1971), *The Long Goodbye* (1973), *Nashville* (1975), and *Three Women* (1977), all acclaimed films, though not altogether popular with audiences.

After years as a major box office draw, Clint Eastwood stepped behind the camera for the first time with *Play Misty for Me* (1971) and displayed an assured, confident hand. *The Outlaw Josey Wales* (1976) was his best film of the decade. He would slowly become one of the finest directors in modern cinema, eventually winning two Academy Awards for Best Director.

Bob Fosse famously directed outstanding films about what happens behind the scenes in entertainment. He bested Francis Ford Coppola for the Best Director Academy Award with *Cabaret* (1972) when Coppola was the favourite to win. He continued with two further nominations for *Lenny* (1974) and *All That Jazz* (1979).

Studio journeyman Franklin J. Shaffner scored a hit with *Planet of the Apes* in 1968 before winning Best Picture and Best Director for *Patton* (1970), kicking off the 70s. He followed the Oscar win with *Nicholas and Alexandra* (1971), a solid biography of the last Russian Tsar, and the superb *Islands in the Stream* (1977), a Hemingway-esque tale with George C. Scott in one of his finest performances.

George Roy Hill was a solid craftsman, a studio's dream coming in on budget and on time film after film. His career exploded in 1969 with *Butch Cassidy and the Sundance Kid*. It continued into the '70s with *The Sting* (1973), which won him an Oscar for Best Director, followed by *The Great Waldo Pepper* (1975) and the sensational comedy *Slap Shot* (1977).

From Italy came Lina Wertmüller, who became the first woman nominated for a Best Director Academy Award with her film *Seven Beauties* (1975). That film, considered her masterpiece, was preceded by *Swept Away* (1974), an equally brilliant film.

Finally, Terrence Malick came out of nowhere with the critically acclaimed films *Badlands* (1973), a superb directing debut, and *Days of Heaven* (1978). After that, he stepped away from directing for twenty years, returning in the 90s with *The Thin Red Line* (1998), his epic war film.

Many others, honing their skills in the 70s, emerged as a new generation of directors in the 80s.

98 THE CONVERSATION (1974)

DIRECTED BY Francis Ford Coppola
COUNTRY USA

Opposite Gene Hackman had few lines to work with but keeps our interest throughout.

By 1974 every American citizen knew what a wiretap was. The Watergate scandal had monopolized the headlines for years, and the "Nixon tapes" became the smoking gun that brought him down. The tapes included everything from conversations about national security to routine discussions between colleagues, leaving no trust when it was all revealed.

The Conversation is a superb character study of Harry Caul, a professional surveillance expert or "bugger" who earns a lucrative income listening and recording the conversations of others.

Yet he pays the price.

He has no life outside of his work. He lives alone and works with one other man, a trusted colleague, but they never seem to socialize. He is paranoid, terrified of having the tables turned on him, becoming the prey rather than the stalker.

Caul (Gene Hackman) is hired to record some conversations and thinks he knows where it is all going but has no idea that he is being used as an alibi for a murder. Discovering the truth, he tears his apartment apart, looking for devices, feeling firsthand the damage he has done to others. To his surprise, he finds he has developed a conscience, a liability in his line of work.

In a nearly silent performance, Gene Hackman is extraordinary, his body language and facial expressions suggesting his intense loneliness, sadness, and paranoia. Yet through it all, he is professional. When he speaks, the words are carefully chosen, precise, and hushed. He realizes too late that his actions have brought about a death.

John Cazale is excellent and equally quiet as his trusted assistant, and Robert Duvall and Cindy Williams shine in minor roles.

Francis Ford Coppola directed this film for under $2 million, in between *The Godfather* (1972) and *The Godfather Part II* (1974), shooting the picture in twenty-eight days, a shoestring project. The reviews were sensational, and come Oscar time, Coppola found himself twice nominated by the Directors Guild of America for their DGA Award, for this and *The Godfather Part II* (for which he won), along with Academy Awards for Best Picture and Best Screenplay.

All four films he directed in the 70s are genuine masterpieces.

"In a nearly silent performance, Gene Hackman is extraordinary, his body language and facial expressions suggesting his intense loneliness, sadness, and paranoia."

100 THE GODFATHER PART II (1974)

DIRECTED BY Francis Ford Coppola
COUNTRY USA

Opposite Michael Corleone (Al Pacino) confronts his brother Fredo (John Cazale) with his betrayal.

Hailed by critics as the finest American film since *Citizen Kane* (1941) and *On the Waterfront* (1954), Coppola's masterpiece about the Corleone crime family was an astounding accomplishment. Seeing the success of the first film, the executives at Paramount almost at once began planning a sequel. Coppola initially resisted but finally, tempted by the challenge (not to mention the money, control, and power over the film), Coppola signed on. He and writer Mario Puzo, author of the book and co-writer of *The Godfather*, returned to the novel to create a second film.

The Godfather Part II bookends the first film, which chronologically becomes the middle story of the Corleone family saga. Many fans refuse to acknowledge *The Godfather Part III* (1990). For me, the end of the Corleone saga ends with Michael alone at the end of Part II.

Coppola and Puzo relied heavily on the novel for the plot of Part II, particularly for Vito's journey to America after the slaughter of his family by a vicious Sicilian Don. The film unfolds in a broken narrative between Vito's meagre beginnings and Michael, his son, in Nevada in 1958. At the end of the first film, Michael, having assumed the role of Don for the Corleones, is moving his family to Las Vegas. Years have passed, and he has consolidated his position further as one of the most influential and ruthless Mafia chieftains.

The two men are juxtaposed. Vito (portrayed superbly by Robert De Niro) is generous and warm, drawing people to him naturally; though wary, he is always willing to do a favour. But we soon learn he is ready to kill his enemies if necessary. Michael is cold, calculating, with the deadly stare of a cobra, and has no trouble ordering the executions of his many enemies. He tells his trusted advisor Tom Hagen (Robert Duvall), "If history has shown us anything, it is that you can kill anyone."

After an assassin nearly kills him and his wife, Kay (Diane Keaton), he searches for the traitor within his family. He knows who gave the order, but someone within the family had to allow access to the Lake Tahoe property with machine guns. He is devastated to learn it was his older brother Fredo (John Cazale).

Meanwhile, Vito takes his revenge on the Don in Sicily, now a doddering old man, while Michael orders the death of Fredo. As for Hyman Roth (Lee Strasberg), the man who engineered the hit on Michael? He is gunned down at an airport while under heavy guard, proving Michael's point that you truly can kill anyone.

The film explores the theme of the corrupting force of absolute power but also, like the first film, looks at the perversity of the American dream. The Corleones pursue a new life through hard work, of course. But the crime element also allowed them to excel beyond their wildest dreams. Coppola also brilliantly shows the power and reach of the Mafia as Roth tells Michael while in Cuba, "Mike, we're bigger than US Steel."

Pacino has never been this astounding. His remarkable performance as Michael, a man slowly selling his soul, was robbed of the Best Actor Oscar award. As young Vito, Robert De Niro may have had the greatest challenge of all, replacing no less than Marlon Brando, who had won an Oscar portraying him in the first film. We see suggestions of Brando in his performance, but he makes the character his own. The cast includes fine performances by Robert Duvall, John Cazale, Diane Keaton, Lee Strasberg, Michael V. Gazzo, and Talia Shire.

Coppola offers his signature extraordinary images: immigrants slowly passing the Statue of Liberty as they land at Ellis Island; the bustling streets of Little Italy early in the twentieth century; Vito killing Fanucci and the cloth around his gun catching fire.

He also gave us unforgettable moments: Vito returning to Sicily to kill the man who murdered his family; the senate hearings in which Michael again wields his enormous power;

"Coppola's film never steps false, a perfect work of art."

Michael's slow realization that it was Fredo, kissing him on the mouth, saying, "I know it was you, Fredo. You broke my heart."; the sad death of Fredo; and finally, Michael alone with the autumn leaves, forever morally corrupt. Both an epic with a vast scope and yet an intimate film, Coppola's movie never steps false, a perfect work of art. It is utterly flawless.

The film was nominated for eleven Academy Awards and would win six for Best Picture, Best Director, Best Supporting Actor (De Niro), Best Screenplay Adaptation, Best Score (composed by Carmine Coppola, father to Francis and Talia Shire), and Best Art Direction. Many critics and historians, this one included, believe the film to be a greater accomplishment than the first. *The Godfather Part II* can truly lay claim to being the greatest American film ever made.

102 THE GREAT GATSBY (1974)

DIRECTED BY Jack Clayton
COUNTRY USA

Opposite Mia Farrow and Robert Redford failed to create sparks together.

If you have a love story with no heat between the lovers, you have nothing.

The failure of *The Great Gatsby* proved that no matter the names on the marquee or the size of the marketing budget, if the film did not work, sophisticated audiences of the 70s would stay away.

Paramount's first challenge was finding the right cast. Everyone had an opinion on who should play the iconic roles in F. Scott Fitzgerald's beloved novel.

Robert Redford was among the top box office draws in the world, just coming off an incredible 1973 with *The Way We Were* and *The Sting*, which had won the Academy Award for Best Picture. Redford was always a fine actor, but could he bring to Gatsby the inherent danger needed for the character that either Warren Beatty or Jack Nicholson could have?

Worse was the casting of Mia Farrow as Daisy. Among the many options considered were Ali MacGraw, Katharine Ross, Jane Fonda, Jill Clayburgh, and Faye Dunaway. Finally, they chose Farrow, thinking she had what it took to bring Daisy to the screen. Only she did not.

She and Redford had zero chemistry. In the book, she and Gatsby are crazy for each other, but she marries a wealthy man instead when Gatsby is away at war. The boorish Tom Buchanan (Bruce Dern) is flush with old family money but has none of Gatsby's sensitivity or romantic appeal. Years go by, and Gatsby moves across the bay from Daisy and Tom. He is now a man of means, but his secrecy about his money, the strange phone calls, and being called away by his "man" strongly suggest his wealth came from nefarious ties. Even though married, Daisy makes no secret of her love for Gatsby, but her very shallowness comes to light when the group goes to New York for a day's outing. A terrible accident kills Tom's lover on the way home, and Tom tells her husband it was Gatsby driving the car which struck her. It was not; it was Daisy. The husband kills Gatsby as he swims in his pool, and Daisy never tells the truth. She and Tom prepare for a trip abroad, and for the first time, we see that Daisy is the perfect match for Tom.

Francis Ford Coppola wrote the screenplay for the film, and Jack Clayton was hired to direct. But despite that lineup, audiences and critics hated it, save for the superb performance of Bruce Dern as Tom, the arrogant, bombastic rich man. Though nominated for a Golden Globe as Best Supporting Actor, Dern failed to crack the Oscar list.

The harshest reviews were directed at Farrow, Redford, and director Clayton in that order. Farrow brought nothing remotely likable to Daisy, so how could Redford, as Gatsby, love her? Redford looked great in the superb costumes, but he and Farrow have no spark. He also fails to capture the complexity of Fitzgerald's character and what drives him to such extremes to win back his love. It is an empty performance, one of the weakest of his career.

Dern gives the film its only energy and seems an unstoppable force whenever on screen, which sadly is not enough. He might have been a better choice for Gatsby. Where is it written that Gatsby must be pretty, even prettier than Daisy? He needed to portray danger, and a hint of sadness wrapped up in a handsome package. Redford did not.

The film, as expected, won a single Academy Award for its excellent costume design.

One aside. From time to time, actors show who they really are beneath the skin of the performance they are giving. Has Mia Farrow ever been more truthful than she is in the closing moments of the film, smugly, even blissfully ignoring what she has done, comfortable with the fact that Gatsby is dead, and her life will go on without a catch? One of the reasons I believe Woody Allen in the sickening allegations Farrow made against him is that she portrayed that moment so well here and in court.

Sadly, one of the notable failures of the decade.

"The harshest reviews were directed at Farrow, Redford, and director Clayton in that order."

104 YOUNG FRANKENSTEIN (1974)

DIRECTED BY Mel Brooks
COUNTRY USA

Opposite The hilarious cast included Teri Garr, Gene Wilder, and Peter Boyle as the monster.

Zany. This word best describes *Young Frankenstein*, the finest of the Mel Brooks parodies from the 1970s and 80s. The film parody genre came about when Mel Brooks made *Blazing Saddles* (1973), an irreverent, satiric western. Brooks created a film that was respectful to the western but poked fun at the same time; affectionate, glorious fun.

While shooting *Blazing Saddles*, actor Gene Wilder discussed a parody of the classic Universal Frankenstein franchise of the 30s. Brooks was interested as long as they agreed to make the film in black and white. Wilder had already been writing the film, so the two men began combing through the Frankenstein films, preferring those with the great Boris Karloff as the monster: *Frankenstein* (1931), *The Bride of Frankenstein* (1935), and *Son of Frankenstein* (1939).

Gene Wilder was a unique comedian, one of the few who could go from absolute calm to raging mania in a millisecond and make it believable. He even looked funny with his wild, dancing eyes and hair. He was the obvious choice for Dr. Frankenstein, grandson of the creature's creator, who has spent most of his life declaring that his grandfather was crazy and that he wants nothing to do with the family legacy.

But drawn to his grandfather's castle and thus the experiments, he begins working in the lab with Igor (pronounced "Eye-gor"), played with madcap genius by wild-eyed Marty Feldman. He discovers his grandfather had indeed learned to bring the dead back to life, which he mistakenly takes for giving life. The great irony of the book that most miss is that Frankenstein never gave life; he brought the dead back to life, corrupted within. And he does the same, creating a childlike monster who, if afraid or angered, becomes dangerous. When Igor stole the brain, he took one marked "Abnormal," which he read as "Abby Normal."

Portrayed by Peter Boyle, this monster is often hilarious as the creature. Watch him reach for the music he believes floats in the air while listening to it, or singing and dancing with Dr. Frankenstein later, massacring the famous tune "Puttin' on the Ritz." His finest moments come when the creature encounters an elderly blind hermit (Gene Hackman) in the woods. The hermit unwittingly harms the monster, pouring hot soup in his lap, smashing his drink mug, and setting his thumb afire, attempting to light a cigar. The creature runs away, terrified of more torture.

The comedy is inspired by the original films, but the two comic minds rework the material, creating hysterically original content. The timeless moments are too numerous to name, but the best include the hunchbacked Igor saying, "What hump?," Dr. Frankenstein's out-of-control rants to God, and the song and dance routine. Frau Blücher (Cloris Leachman) endures the whinnying of horses whenever her name is mentioned and explodes with the line about Frankenstein's grandfather, "YES! He... was... my... BOYFRIEND!!"

The brilliant black and white cinematography provides the look of the classic Universal monster movies and the German Expressionistic period. They do not come any funnier than this film. Mel Brooks told his cast never to play it funny; let the comedy emerge rather than force it. Of course, his direction was spot-on. A superb company of actors brought life to the screenplay. When production was over, none wanted to leave because they were having so much fun.

None of the actors received nominations, but it was a tough race that year for Academy Awards. It was nominated for the superb Screenplay and for Sound, but nothing else.

Too bad because many of the actors were highly deserving. Wilder, Leachman, Garr, and Boyle were all worthy of discussion for Oscar nominations; even Gene Hackman's tiny unbilled role as the blind man remains a comic gem.

Is *Young Frankenstein* the best comedy of the 70s? It just might be.

"Mel Brooks told his cast never to play it funny; let the comedy emerge rather than force it. Of course, his direction was spot-on."

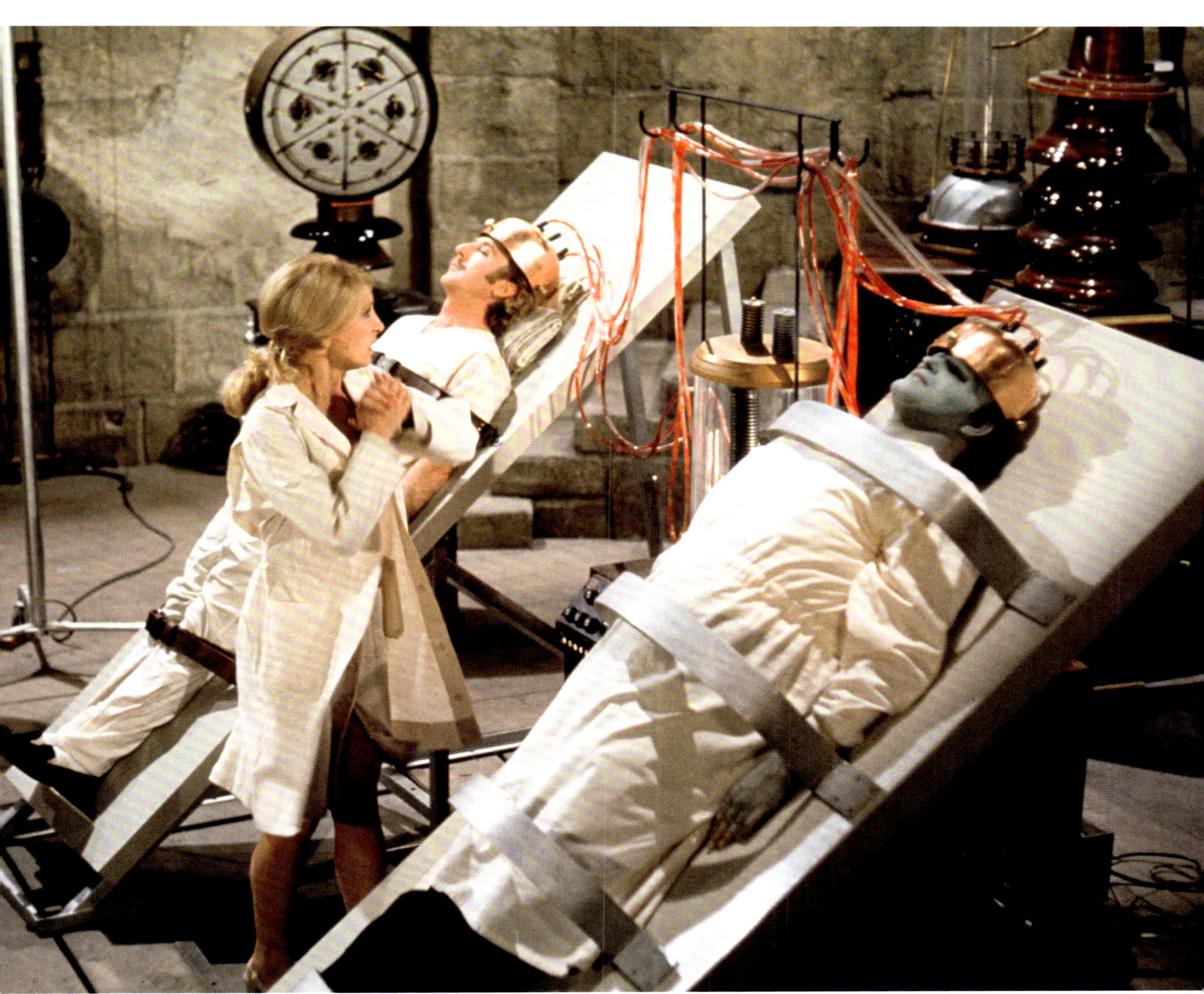

106

"Of all his painstaking work, *Barry Lyndon* is Kubrick at his finest and most meticulous."

BARRY LYNDON (1975)

DIRECTED BY Stanley Kubrick
COUNTRY USA/United Kingdom

The best way to watch a Kubrick film is to give in, allow yourself to experience it, and be open to the whole sensory, luxurious experience.

The Academy Awards has a long history of ignoring Stanley Kubrick. He has been in the running four times, for *Barry Lyndon*, *Dr. Strangelove* (1964), *2001: A Space Odyssey* (1968), and again for *A Clockwork Orange* (1971), but has never won. Despite his empty trophy case, he is often hailed as one of cinema's greatest filmmakers.

Many would rate Kubrick's exquisitely beautiful film *Barry Lyndon* as his finest work. When first released, it earned rave reviews from some critics, but was dismissed as a slow-moving dud by others. The plot may be slow, but there is no denying the startling images the director and cinematographer John Alcott achieved. It was as though a time machine had transported them back to the 1700s to shoot a documentary rather than a narrative feature film. The sheer artistry of the cinematography is enough to bring you to tears. Each shot looks like a painting of the time. Of all his painstaking work, *Barry Lyndon* is Kubrick at his finest and most meticulous.

Kubrick shot the film mostly in Ireland over three hundred days, a very long shooting schedule. His crew was devoted to him, believing in his vision to create the most realistic film set in the 1700s. The countryside of Ireland looks untouched and pristine in every way. The indoor candlelight scenes are luminous, and the entire film feels like one single take of exquisite grace. Kubrick had learned about new lenses that NASA was testing out. He managed to borrow some, and the results are stunning.

Ryan O'Neal plays Redmond Barry, who will marry into the name Lyndon and set about spending his wife's fortune with wild abandon. A degenerate gambler and hopeless womanizer, he does not even try to hide his many affairs. Eventually, her son Lord Bullingdon provokes a vicious fight with him in public that ruins any chance of Barry receiving a title. Young Bullingdon leaves but returns and challenges Barry to a duel to the death. When the young man's pistol discharges and misfires, Barry refuses to shoot at him in return. The boy responds by shooting Barry in the leg, which must be amputated. Hoping to end the matter, Bullingdon offers Barry a settlement of money to leave. Broken by life, the shattering death of his other young son, and his failure to find a place in society, he does indeed go away.

O'Neal was never a great actor, but he was very popular in the early 70s after his performance in *Love Story* (1970) and work with Peter Bogdanovich in the comedies *What's Up Doc?* (1971) and *Paper Moon* (1973). Some questioned Kubrick's decision to cast O'Neal, but time has been very kind to the performance. He brings to the role a caddish element, enough to make audiences dislike him, so they do not get emotionally attached to him.

O'Neal knew he was a pawn in a Kubrick production, but he happily went along, though the endless shooting bothered him. The actor captures Barry's eventual downfall, which seems earned, having been less than an honourable gentleman his entire life. His fall from grace comes slowly, and by the time it is over, he has nothing left, not even his dignity.

The film received mixed reviews, though it won the New York Film Critics Awards for Best Picture and Best Director that year. *Barry Lyndon* was subsequently nominated for seven Academy Awards and would win four, for Best Cinematography, Best Costume Design, Best Art Direction, and Best Adapted Score. Kubrick was nominated for a Directors Guild of America Award but lost. He would have to settle for making timeless films.

Opposite Ryan O'Neal and Marisa Berenson in their award-winning costumes.

"Knowing the performances of Pacino and Cazale were crucial, he focuses on them."

DOG DAY AFTERNOON (1975)

DIRECTED BY Sidney Lumet
COUNTRY USA

It began like any sweltering day in New York City during a heat wave.

Three well-dressed guys walk into a bank, one carrying a large box of flowers. As soon as they are inside, one backs out of whatever they are planning and runs. One of the remaining two approaches the cashier. He fumbles with the box but then pulls out a rifle and points it at the terrified cashier. The other one has a gun too. They mean business. But the bank is low on cash, and the cops across the street are calling.

Anything can happen in New York on a dog day afternoon.

So, they take hostages and begin making demands, threatening to start killing the hostages if the police don't comply. Sonny (Al Pacino) does most of the talking, and his friend Sal (John Cazale) is the more threatening of the two, continually reminding Sonny that he's ready to shoot. As if Sonny did not have enough trouble, he needs to worry about his unleashed partner.

Very quickly, Sonny turns the robbery into a circus, showboating outside when speaking with the police, bringing the crowd to chant "Attica!! Attica!" in reference to the police violence at the New York prison the year before. Sonny shines in the limelight, and it worries the police.

Then the police deliver Leon (Chris Sarandon), Sonny's lover. They learn that Sonny robbed the bank to pay for Leon's sex change operation. No one is more shocked at this development than Sonny's hysterical wife. Sal is unimpressed because the media is saying, "two homosexuals are robbing the bank." *The Boys in the Band* (1970) was the first major film to deal openly with homosexuality, followed by *Sunday, Bloody Sunday* (1971). *Dog Day Afternoon* was next, with Pacino being the first major Hollywood actor to portray an openly bisexual man. At the time, this was considered a bold, daring choice for him.

The plot builds until the bus is delivered and Sonny and Sal are headed to the airport along with the hostages. Suddenly, and it happens so fast, Sal is dead, shot in the head, and Sonny is in handcuffs.

Their day began with so much promise!

Sidney Lumet directed *Dog Day Afternoon* with the perfect amount of drama and comedy, much of it very droll, and it works like a dream. His camera roams the crowded streets outside the bank, focuses on Sonny's strutting and captures the growing claustrophobia inside the bank. Knowing the performances of Pacino and Cazale were crucial, he focuses on them. Pacino is genuinely magnificent, whether showboating for the crowds or quietly talking to the hostages about what has driven him to this.

Cazale is a revelation, blankly answering "Wyoming" when Sonny asks him where he wants to go when they get out of here. In his few minutes of screen time, Chris Sarandon is superb as Leon, Sonny's lover, casting a whole new light on Sonny's motives.

The film was an immediate hit with audiences and critics, topping many ten best lists and battling *One Flew Over the Cuckoo's Nest* (1975) for the top of those lists. Nominated for six Academy Awards, including Best Picture, Best Actor (Pacino), Best Director, and Best Supporting Actor (Sarandon), the film won only a single award, for its Screenplay.

Al Pacino was extraordinary through the 70s but was prone to shouting his parts later in his career. After the failure of *Revolution* (1985), he walked away from film for three years. So sad, because *The Godfather* (1972), *The Godfather Part II* (1974), *Serpico* (1973), and *Dog Day Afternoon* (1975) remain compelling reminders of how gifted an actor he truly was in his prime.

Opposite Sonny (Al Pacino) decides on his next move as he holds a bank at gunpoint.

110 JAWS (1975)

DIRECTED BY Steven Spielberg
COUNTRY USA

Opposite Steven Spielberg in the jaws of his troublesome mechanical shark.

The young woman swims out into the tranquil, glassy ocean, beautifully lit by the moon. We see her nude body treading underwater, ominous music building. Without warning, she disappears. She comes to the surface in panic but is pulled under again. This time, when she resurfaces, she lets out a blood-curdling scream. She is being torn apart by a shark and thrown around the water like a rag doll. Then, silence. The calm water returns. It was as if she was never there.

Jaws opened with mediocre expectations, yet the film would spark a cultural phenomenon in the days, weeks, and months after its release. Based on the book by Peter Benchley, Universal gave the directing job to atwenty-six-year-old newcomer named Steven Spielberg, who had directed one other feature film, *The Sugarland Express* (1974), and some acclaimed television films including *Duel* (1971).

The decision to shoot on the ocean was a controversial and unpopular one, as previous ocean shoots had typically been problematic for the crew and cast. Continuity could be brutal because of the ever-changing clouds, but that wasn't even the worst part. They built three mechanical sharks for the film, and two promptly sank to the bottom of the sea. Over the walkie-talkies, it became commonplace to hear, "The shark is not working."

So, Spielberg got creative. Blessed with an extraordinary imagination, he decided to show less of the shark than described in the screenplay, using the Hitchcock adage that less was more. He would suggest the shark's presence throughout the film and finally reveal the massive beast closer to the end, when it was essential. His creativity saved the film and made it the masterpiece of terror it would become. Despite going way over budget, Universal stuck by their young director, believing he had something.

When the film opened in 1975, no one, including Universal, was prepared for the madness that ensued. Audience queues snaked for hours around city blocks as screenings sold out quickly. The unanimously positive reviews added to the enthusiasm. Shark mania swept North America. Spielberg had created something extraordinary, a modern-day horror film with a monster we all might encounter one day. It made the film's story plausible and, therefore, genuinely terrifying.

We see two shark attacks without ever seeing the shark. The second is a little boy playing on his air mattress, attacked while swimming near a crowded beach. We see a geyser of blood and then mayhem. Finally, the town's mayor, who has been trying to quell the panic, agrees to send a trio to kill the shark. Brody (Roy Scheider), Hooper (Richard Dreyfuss), and Quint (Robert Shaw) bravely board Quint's vessel and head out to sea to find the shark and kill it.

The screenplay is deceptive in its depth, with a simple plotline. Three men go shark hunting. But the superb performances and Spielberg's perfect direction make the film a terrifying nail-biter. You never know what is coming next. Oddly, despite the brutality and horror of the shark attacks, the most frightening scene in the film is Quint describing his experiences on the SS *Indianapolis*. This WWII ship was sunk after delivering the Hiroshima bomb. The men floated for days before being rescued, and many succumbed to shark attacks while their friends watched in horror. We know at once why Quint hates sharks.

Before the summer of 1975 was over, *Jaws* was the highest money maker in film history, surpassing *The Godfather* (1972) in a few short months. Nominated for just four Academy Awards, it would win Best Sound, Best Film Editing, and Best Musical Score for John Williams's now iconic music. His score contributed to the success of the film as much as anything the director did. It lost Best Picture and, criminally, Spielberg was not a nominee for Best Director; nor were Robert Shaw for Best Supporting Actor, the film's Cinematography, or Visual Effects. All ignored.

"*Jaws* revolutionized the horror genre with its realism."

Like *Psycho* (1960), *Jaws* revolutionized the horror genre with its realism. Throughout the summer of 1975, swimmers refused to go into the ocean, even lakes and ponds!

And Spielberg became a household name overnight and went on to be one of the greatest directors in the history of cinema, with *Jaws* still among his finest films. One co-worker, marvelling at his brilliance, said, "the ideas just poured off of him, and if they did not work, he moved on." He would direct some of the most beloved films of all time, including *Close Encounters of the Third Kind* (1977), *Raiders of the Lost Ark* (1981), *E.T. the Extra-Terrestrial* (1982), and *Jurassic Park* (1993), before directing his masterpiece *Schindler's List* (1993), which would win seven Academy Awards and finally win him his Best Director Oscar. He continues to dazzle audiences today and has earned his place among the great directors of all time, possibly at the very top of that list.

"While it certainly has moments that soar, it is too inconsistent to be declared a masterpiece."

NASHVILLE (1975)

DIRECTED BY Robert Altman
COUNTRY USA

After seeing an advance cut of Robert Altman's *Nashville*, film critic Pauline Kael responded with a long, detailed review in *The New Yorker*, where she declared the film the finest made in the United States in many years. She elevated Altman to near rock star with her glowing review, and while audiences waited to see the premiere, the editors were whittling it down to a releasable length. Cinema chains do not care for films longer than three hours because it limits the number of showings. So, Altman was pressured to cut a significant portion from the original that Kael glowingly reviewed. Did Kael ever see the shortened version that went into cinemas? Likely, but regardless, the version in her review never made it to the final screen.

Like the best Altman films, this one contains the characteristics that came to define his work: the overlapping dialogue, a large cast of characters with connected stories, and some form of social satire. Granted, it has staying power, so you will find yourself revisiting the scenes long after the movie ends. And while it certainly has moments that soar, it is too inconsistent to be declared a masterpiece.

At his best, Altman was an inventive filmmaker beloved by actors for his habit of letting them improvise, thereby drawing on their own ideas. Actors love being part of the creative process, and Altman was never too controlling or insecure to allow them to participate. He challenged actors to be creative.

When *Nashville* was released, Altman had made just three exciting films, one of them *M*A*S*H* (1970), a truly great film. *McCabe & Mrs. Miller* (1971) was interesting but flawed, and *The Long Goodbye* (1973) divided audiences and critics.

Nashville was equally divisive, though critics embraced it. The film explores the humiliations people will go through for stardom, and the trappings of celebrity. Over a few days, the movie is immersed in a music festival in Nashville, the country and western capital of the world. Wannabe country stars are everywhere, narratives interconnect, and a shattering event instantly involves all the characters.

Among the finer performances are Henry Gibson (best known as a comic on *Laugh-In*) as a pretentious singer; Lily Tomlin as the mother of deaf children who has an affair with womanizing singer Keith Carradine; and best of all, Ronee Blakley as a doomed country singer who is met with an assassin's bullet. Geraldine Chaplin is excellent as an ambitious and relentless journalist for the BBC, and Barbara Harris is equally superb as an opportunistic singer who grabs the microphone and sings after the shooting.

Nashville tied for Best Picture with *Barry Lyndon* for the New York Film Critics Award, and was nominated for five Academy Awards, including Best Picture, Best Director, and Supporting Actress (Blakley). It did win an Oscar for the song "I'm Easy" by Carradine. Hailed an American masterpiece, it divided critics then and continues to do so today. That said, it might be Altman's finest film.

Opposite Karen Black as Connie White belts out a tune.

114 ONE FLEW OVER THE CUCKOO'S NEST (1975)

DIRECTED BY Miloš Forman
COUNTRY USA

Opposite Jack Nicholson in the heartbreaking final moments.

Kirk Douglas had long owned the rights to the book *One Flew Over the Cuckoo's Nest*, written by Ken Kesey, but had never managed to make it into a film. He did bring the work to Broadway, taking the lead role of Randle P. McMurphy for himself, but finally gave up on making a film and gifted the rights to his son Michael, then a rising TV star. The younger Douglas went outside the movie business for the funds to make the film, approaching record producer Saul Zaentz, who owned Fantasy Records.

Douglas decided on Czech director Miloš Forman, believing his realistic touch would add measurably to the film. Many lead actors turned down Jack Nicholson's role, including Marlon Brando, Gene Hackman, and James Caan. Jane Fonda, Anne Bancroft, and Ellen Burstyn all turned down the part of Nurse Ratched before Louise fletcher, a supporting actress in some Robert Altman films, took the role. The Oregon State mental hospital and some of its patients feature prominently in the film.

The movie received glowing reviews and quickly became a major success, finding recognition as an American great. Forman's film explored the institutional process with a strong critique of psychiatry as well as a study of corruption of power, all while asking the question, which is worse, the patients or those running the institution?

Despising authority, R.P. McMurphy (Nicholson) arrives at the hospital feigning mental illness to get out of serving on a work detail while in prison for statutory rape. He immediately locks horns with the tyrannical Nurse Ratched (Fletcher), who runs her ward with an iron fist. The rebellious McMurphy quickly realizes that she has emasculated the men with manipulation and threats and goes to work to end her reign of terror on the men. He does not realize until later that she can hold him here as long as she wants; she can arbitrarily choose to extend his remaining jail term of sixty-eight days. Stunned at this revelation, McMurphy then discovers that most of the men on the ward are voluntary, able to walk out whenever they want.

McMurphy's efforts to prove to the men they can be free of Ratched come at a cost. Billy Bibbit (Brad Dourif) is a stuttering young man for whom McMurphy arranges a first sexual encounter with a woman. In return, Ratched threatens and belittles him enough that he kills himself, cutting his throat when left alone in an office. McMurphy goes beserk and attacks Ratched, strangling her until being knocked out by the guards. Ratched has him lobotomized, and he returns a vegetable. Chief Bromden (Will Sampson), a towering Native American, watches it all unfold and sets McMurphy free, smothering him with a pillow before his own dramatic departure.

The soaring ending to the film will stay with you.

Jack Nicholson was breathtaking as McMurphy, the greatest performance of his long career, while Louise Fletcher was superb as the calm, quietly terrifying nurse. The fine supporting cast, including Brad Dourif (Bibbit), Danny DeVito (Martini), William Redfield (Harding), Sydney Lassick (Cheswick), and Will Sampson (Chief) comprise one of the best ensembles in film history.

One Flew Over the Cuckoo's Nest became the first film in forty-one years to sweep the major Academy Awards, winning Best Picture, Best Actor (Nicholson), Best Actress (Fletcher), Best Director (Forman), and Best Screenplay Adaptation, a feat not accomplished since 1934 with *It Happened One Night*. Nicholson swept the year's Best Actor awards, adding to his cache of awards from the National Society of Film Critics and New York Film Critics, as well as the Golden Globe. Forman collected the Directors Guild of America Award for

"Widely considered one of the greatest American films, both a box office smash and critical hit."

his superb direction and the film swept the annual British Academy Awards, adding Best Supporting Actor for Brad Dourif.

Widely considered one of the greatest American films, both a box office smash and critical hit, *One Flew Over the Cuckoo's Nest* remains a stunning work of art.

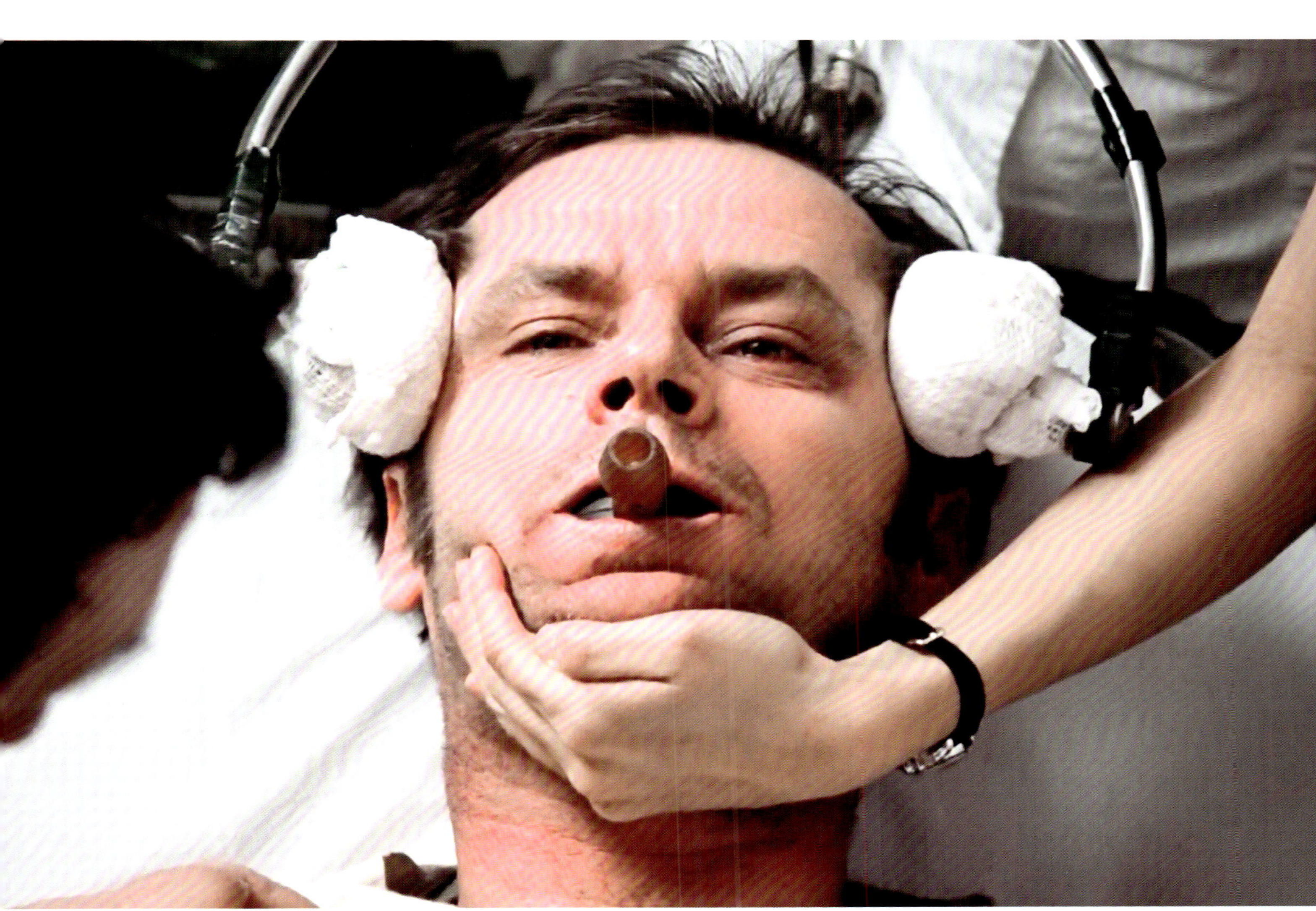

“Antonioni was not known as an actor’s director, but Nicholson was confident it would work out.”

THE PASSENGER (1975)

DIRECTED BY Michelangelo Antonioni
COUNTRY Italy

Jack Nicholson had a hectic year in 1975, with four major films released, the final one earning him a richly deserved Academy Award for Best Actor (*One Flew Over the Cuckoo's Nest*). Long a fan of director Antonioni, Nicholson was delighted when the gifted filmmaker offered a role in his new film, *The Passenger*. Antonioni was not known as an actor's director, but Nicholson was confident it would work out.

Maria Schneider would be his co-star, fresh from success in *Last Tango in Paris* two years earlier. Her success working with Brando in that controversial film further excited Nicholson about working with her.

When released, the film seemed to confound audiences, who expected something different from Nicholson, by now a much-loved actor best known for his rebellious characters who disdain authority. His character in *The Passenger* is the most introspective one the actor has ever portrayed.

As David Locke, a well-known reporter working for the British media, Nicholson portrays an unassuming man who, despite his fame as a television journalist, prefers a quiet life. When a man dies in his hotel room in Northern Chad, Locke assumes the man's identity and allows the world and his grieving wife to believe he is dead. We never really know why he wants to disappear, only that he takes an enormous risk to do so. The dead man whose life Locke assumes is Robertson, an arms dealer to the local rebels fighting a civil war. After keeping an appointment with one of the rebels in the dead man's book, he is given a large packet of cash for arms he cannot provide.

He and a character known only as the Girl (Schneider) take off across the country, freely spending their ill-gotten gains. It does not take long for the rebels to realize they were scammed and begin to search for Locke, and of course, they find him.

Locke is neither as boisterous nor outgoing as other characters Nicholson has portrayed. Still, he is entirely invested and at home playing this different role and gives a fine performance. Schneider is adequate, certainly less erotic than with Brando.

Emptiness, a metaphor for his life, is all around Locke. The opening sequence, where his jeep gets stuck in the vast desert, and he is alone and isolated, reflects his life's situation.

Antonioni was a master of atmosphere and making the landscape a secondary character. He does so here superbly, though the film did not attract audiences as the two men had hoped. It was Nicholson's first bomb in quite some time, but it didn't take him long to recover.

Opposite Jack Nicholson and Maria Schneider during their brief romance.

THE ROCKY HORROR PICTURE SHOW (1975)

DIRECTED BY Jim Sharman
COUNTRY USA

Opposite Outlandish make-up and costumes were de rigueur in this classic film with Tim Curry.

Alan Parker's *Fame* (1980) includes a scene that helps to explain the Rocky Horror experience. The students at a performing arts school in New York City have gathered to see the midnight screening of *The Rocky Horror Picture Show*. They act out the film as it plays. Someone in the audience screams to get on with the show, and a kid calls back, "We are the fucking show!"

He was exactly right.

Though it bombed badly upon its initial release, midnight screenings and a massive cult following made *The Rocky Horror Show* one of the most popular, beloved films of the 70s and 80s. There are still midnight screenings, where the packed audience dresses as the characters, the bravest of them acting out entire scenes. They shout lines, sing, comment, dance, and use props to react to what's happening on the screen. It really is an experience.

At a modest cost of $1.6 million, the film has brought in more than $230 million, a massive return for 20th Century Fox, now owned by Disney.

The film explores what happens when a pair of innocents wander into the castle of Dr. Frank-N-Furter (Tim Curry) and end up staying as his "guests." They first encounter his trusty servant Riff Raff (Richard O'Brien), who dances "The Time Warp" with his sister before introducing them to the great doctor. Like Frankenstein before him, he has been creating life in his lab. His monster is for his sexual gratification, a well-muscled, tanned young man who decides he is not attracted to men but sure likes the girls. And so it goes with a silly narrative, and some wild twists until Frank-N-Furter is finally killed after being overthrown and ordered back to his home planet.

The film pays homage to horror films such as *Frankenstein* (1931) and *King Kong* (1933). The songs are catchy and fun. "The Time Warp" became an international sensation.

The performances are surprisingly good, especially Tim Curry. With his terrific singing voice and dressed in sexy women's underwear, his entrance into the film is simply electrifying. Curry is bold, confident, and very sexual. I once overheard a man say, "I wouldn't kick him out of bed." Curry had that kind of impact.

Richard O'Brien, who wrote the play and the film, was excellent as Riff Raff, the doctor's loyal (to a point) servant. Meat Loaf has a fantastic scene bursting out of a fridge to sing a rock song, and both Susan Sarandon and Barry Bostwick are the perfect nerds who happen upon the castle and have their lives altered forever.

It is irreverent, brash, and great fun. Is it a work of art? In its own way, it might be. But those who love the film don't care. From the second those huge red lips greet us, we are hooked.

"Don't dream it, be it," the lyrics tell us.

Indeed.

“It is irreverent, brash, and great fun. Is it a work of art? In its own way, it might be.”

"Together they were magic as two old vaudevillians invited to appear in a TV special about the history of comedy."

THE SUNSHINE BOYS (1975)

DIRECTED BY Herbert Ross
COUNTRY USA

Neil Simon was the most prolific film and stage writer of his time. After the stage and film successes of *Barefoot in the Park* (1967) and *The Odd Couple* (1968), Simon could do no wrong. In the early 70s, he was the go-to comedy writer but mostly busy with his own work. In 1975, two of his plays were made into successful films.

The Prisoner of Second Avenue spoke to the rising unemployment in the United States. A middle-aged man finds himself out of work, alone in his apartment, slowly having a full-scale breakdown. The role of Mel seemed tailor-made for Jack Lemmon, who made an art form out of portraying the anxiety-ridden meltdown.

The better of his 1975 releases was the wonderful *The Sunshine Boys*, with standout performances from Walter Matthau and George Burns. Together they were magic as two old vaudevillians invited to appear in a TV special about the history of comedy. They have not spoken for many years, having had an ugly breakup years ago, and get off to a terrible start.

Willie (Matthau) is still trying to work but often blows the auditions or goes to the wrong address. He is short-tempered and bombastic and must be convinced to do the show with his former partner, Al Lewis (Burns), a sweet-natured old fellow happily in retirement and living with his daughter since the death of his wife. Though they used to work together almost exclusively, it has been twenty years. Falling right back into the rhythms they had for their comedy sketches is easy, but Willie cannot let go of the past and how Al left. The humour in the film comes from their verbal sparring and the gradual realization of what everybody around them already knows—that they love each other deeply.

The film is a fascinating look at the evolution of sketch comedy, progressing from the inside of small theatres to television. Al and Willie must catch up to the new way of doing things, but change comes hard, especially for the stubborn Willie.

Walter Matthau was a large, lumbering fellow who began his career playing heavies before the world discovered he was a comedic genius. He won an Oscar for Best Supporting Actor as the crooked lawyer in *The Fortune Cookie* (1966) and was nominated for his role as the old man in *Kotch* (1971). His third came for *The Sunshine Boys*, probably the finest performance of his career. Portraying a man twenty years his senior, he is wonderful.

Burns took over the role when Jack Benny withdrew, diagnosed with pancreatic cancer (he would be gone by the end of the year). The chemistry with George Burns, best known as a radio star, is superb. Droll, gentle, and quiet, Burns is a comic delight as Lewis, and won the Academy Award for Best Supporting Actor, after which he enjoyed a career revival on the big screen.

The Sunshine Boys was a solid hit with audiences, and critics praised their performances. Among Simon's films in the 70s, only *The Goodbye Girl* (1977) was a bigger hit. A remake of *The Sunshine Boys* was made for television starring Woody Allen and Peter Falk but did not come close to the original film.

Opposite Walter Matthau and George Burns as *The Sunshine Boys*.

"Ken Russell was the king of wretched excess, the enfant terrible of modern cinema in the 70s."

TOMMY (1975)

DIRECTED BY Ken Russell
COUNTRY United Kingdom

During a television appearance a few years ago, I was asked to describe in one word the film *Tommy* (1975). I answered without hesitation—"Phantasmagorical," stealing a word from the children's film *Chitty Chitty Bang Bang* (1968). It perfectly describes this wild ride of a musical rock opera.

Ken Russell was the king of wretched excess, the enfant terrible of modern cinema in the 70s. His films were often wildly over the top but always entertaining. His darkest film was *The Devils* (1971), a superb study of the corruption and power of religion. Both *Women in Love* (1969) and *The Music Lovers* (1971) won acclaim for their outstanding performances, and *The Boy Friend* (1971) was a solid adaptation of the stage play.

Tommy, his wildest film of the decade, was adapted from The Who's rock opera and starred a who's who in rock. Tommy (Roger Daltrey) goes deaf, dumb, and blind after witnessing the murder of his birth father by his stepfather, Frank (Oliver Reed). His mother, portrayed brilliantly by Ann-Margret, seeks a cure but foolishly chooses the wrong person to tend to him. Cousin Kevin is a sadistic masochist who enjoys touring Tommy; they visit Uncle Ernie (Keith Moon), a sexual predator who abuses him, and The Acid Queen (Tina Turner), who sends Tommy on a wild trip but does nothing to cure him. Tommy finds fame by becoming the pinball champion of the world, defeating the greatest of them all, portrayed by an electrifying Elton John. Now The Pinball Wizard, he is world famous.

A doctor, portrayed by a leering Jack Nicholson, tries to cure him, more to find favour with his mother, and he too fails. His mother finally heals him when she throws him through a mirror to the ocean below, and he returns to the surface free, able to hear, speak, and see.

Tommy becomes an inspiration to the young of the world, a Christ-like figure, but Frank and his family commercialize him, and the greed with which they do it causes the followers to revolt. Tommy hears them and climbs the mountain, prepared to be the symbol of hope they need him to be.

It was a first for audiences, a strange film with fast edits, close-ups, and zany cinematography. It profoundly influenced rock videos when they took the industry by storm a few years later with MTV. It was like a wild trip on hallucinogens seeing the beans gushing through the TV onto Ann-Margret's writhing body, the wicked Acid Queen sequence with Tina Turner twitching with withdrawal, and Tommy, with golden locks, climbing the mountain at the end to atone for his greed.

Among the memorable performances, Ann-Margret towers above them with a bold, fierce piece of acting that earned her an Oscar nomination. The music is unforgettable, the songs outstanding, and the rock stars perform them with heart and ferocity. It is an extraordinary experience and not easily forgotten.

Opposite John Entwistle, Roger Daltrey, and Pete Townshend with Elton John in his signature platform boots.

124 1900 (1976)

DIRECTED BY Bernardo Bertolucci
COUNTRY Italy

Opposite Bernardo Bertolucci's massive epic explores family and politics within Italy at the turn of the century.

The original cut of Bertolucci's epic *1900* was one of the finest historical dramas but almost didn't make it to the screen. The first hurdle was selling the five-hour running time to cinemas and audiences. At one point, the reels were even misplaced. Thankfully, Olive Films cut the film back together, restoring the previously cut scenes and releasing all 317 minutes of the film. That is the only version of the film worth reviewing.

Should the work of the great film masters be touched? Certainly not by studio chiefs who know nothing about the art of cinema. Bertolucci gave a purpose to every single moment in *1900*. A masterpiece like this is not a series of scenes; the director plans and sets up every shot long before the actors bring it to life. Variations to plan happen only when actors improvise, something goes terribly wrong with a stunt while the camera is rolling, or a rehearsal is shot unbeknownst to the actors. Making a film is a precise art form, and Bertolucci left nothing to chance. If his film needed to be five hours, his film was going to be five hours.

With an international cast, *1900* tells the stories of two boys, one wealthy, Alfredo (Robert De Niro), the other a peasant, Olmo (Gérard Depardieu), both born on the same day, on the same estate, and who grow up together as friends. The movie explores the first half of the twentieth century, when the war between Fascists and Communists in Italy was at its peak. Bertolucci explores the fanaticism of some political beliefs, or rather that some beliefs inspire, primarily through the character Attila (Donald Sutherland), a cruel, vile, self-serving man. In many ways, the film is a history of Italy and the political strife that the country experienced throughout the two world wars. The impact of the war on individuals is presented in a heart-wrenching manner.

The cast assembled for the film includes the leads mentioned above, De Niro and Depardieu, along with Burt Lancaster, Sterling Hayden, Dominique Sanda, Sutherland, and Laura Betti. No question, the accents of the very different actors cause some issues, but Bertolucci is such a strong visual director he overcomes the obstacles. The great cinematographer Vittorio Storaro shot this film before moving on to his three Oscar-winning creations, *Apocalypse Now* (1979), *Reds* (1981), and *The Last Emperor* (1987), along with many other admirable films. The master of light often worked with Bertolucci, as well as Francis Ford Coppola, Warren Beatty, and later in his career, Woody Allen.

The performances were uniformly strong, with Lancaster a standout as Alfredo's lusty, exuberant father and Sterling Hayden as his friend, the peasant and father of Olmo. Some criticized Donald Sutherland for enjoying playing the psychotic Attila a little too much, a compliment to his authenticity.

Obviously, the film's length limited showings. Many cinemas weren't prepared to offer such a long feature. Thus, it enjoyed limited success despite being hailed as a masterpiece in Italy. Today it is often considered Bertolucci's grand folly. That said, it is an expansive film, epic in scale but balancing the intimacy of its central storyline and the many other narratives woven into the film.

“Making a film is a precise art form, and Bertolucci left nothing to chance. If his film needed to be five hours, his film was going to be five hours.”

A STAR IS BORN (1976)

DIRECTED BY Frank Pierson
COUNTRY USA

Opposite Despite their combined talent, Kristofferson and Streisand weren't convincing as lovers.

Many believe that Judy Garland deserved the Academy Award for Best Actress for her performance in the second version of *A Star Is Born* (1954), but the gifted actress lost to Grace Kelly in *The Country Girl*.

In 1976, when Barbra Streisand played the same role, there was no such talk. Critics universally panned the movie. But audiences adored it, and the oddball Hollywood Foreign Press Association awarded it four Golden Globes, including Best Film (Musical/ Comedy), Best Actor (Musical/Comedy), Best Actress (Musical/Comedy), and Best Song. It was the third incarnation of the movie, and the best was yet to come in 2017, directed by and starring Bradley Cooper with the rock superstar Lady Gaga. Cooper's version was critically acclaimed and nominated for seven Academy Awards.

In the 1976 version, rumours surfaced about the monumental self-indulgence of its star Barbra Streisand, who allegedly bullied and tormented the director, Frank Pierson. Though Streisand had tried to get Elvis Presley to portray the male lead in the film, he begged off, citing ill health. She and partner Jon Peters (now a producer, formerly her hairdresser) approached folk singer Kris Kristofferson to portray the burnt-out rock star, John Norman Howard. Kristofferson agreed, though he probably regretted it as he was often at war with Peters (a ferocious hothead) during the challenging shoot. More than once, the actor nearly came to blows with Peters, who regularly tried to throw his weight around and prove himself.

The story remained very close to the original: a rock star on the way down discovers a talented woman trying to break through, helps her, falls in love with her, marries her, and then begins to be a drag on her career. All those around her tell her to get rid of him, but she loves him. Seeing what he is doing to her, he kills himself, setting her free and ending his own pain.

Kristofferson beautifully plays the sad, drunken Howard, tired of it all, wanting some peace in his life. He is happiest when clearing land for their new house on a bulldozer with Esther (Streisand) playfully helping him. But inevitably, the business creeps back into their lives, and Howard can no longer handle it. Streisand is portraying a variation of her brand, the personality she wants us to believe is her, and it just did not work. There was no spark between the two lovers; without that, the love story wanes.

We get endlessly long, lingering close-ups of Streisand. The camera closes in on her during her final song. For eight agonizing minutes, it's just her. It wore audiences down. Streisand insisted on the shots as her already substantial ego soared out of control.

The soundtrack was superb, with many of the songs by Streisand and Paul Williams, including the Oscar-winning love theme "Evergreen." Though rock was not Kristofferson's milieu, he superbly captured the growl of a burnt-out rock star, often sounding like Bruce Springsteen, who was then emerging as a major force in rock.

When the dust settled, it appeared a star had been born with this movie. Surprisingly, it was Kristofferson.

"There was no spark between the two lovers; without that, the love story wanes."

128 **“William Goldman provided one of the finest screenplays ever written, making sense of a plethora of journalistic and political information.”**

ALL THE PRESIDENT'S MEN (1976)

DIRECTED BY Alan J. Pakula
COUNTRY USA

The resignation of President Richard Nixon sent seismic shock waves through the United States, although it was his only choice. Having forever violated the American people's trust, Nixon was finished politically. Despite his accomplishments and long track record, there was simply no coming back from Watergate. Once Bob Woodward and Carl Bernstein of *The Washington Post* began investigating a break-in at the Watergate Hotel's Democratic headquarters, Nixon was doomed. After being re-elected in 1972 by the largest landslide victory in the history of American elections, just two years later, Nixon resigned.

The two reporters who brought down a presidency documented the story in a superb book, which won a Pulitzer Prize. Actor Robert Redford bought the rights to the book, believing there was a film there. He was exactly right.

William Goldman provided one of the finest screenplays ever written, making sense of a plethora of journalistic and political information. Redford hired Alan J. Pakula to direct the film. The gifted and astute Pakula saw the film as a detective thriller, so he included undertones of paranoia and menace, with the two actors constantly looking over their shoulders to see who, from the White House, was after them.

Redford took the lead role of Woodward, and Dustin Hoffman was Carl Bernstein. Veteran actor Jason Robards played the tough *Washington Post* editor Ben Bradlee, who believed in his reporters but knew there was no room for error. The film opens with the burglary at the Watergate Office Building and moves chronologically through the events that saw the reporters writing the story that would eventually bring Nixon down.

This is likely the best film about journalism, though David Fincher's haunting *Zodiac* (2007) comes close. Woodward and Bernstein's accomplishments occurred before the invention of the internet, back when reporting involved a lot of hard work, dogged research, phone calls, endless dead ends, and interviews with people who didn't want to talk.

There is a magnificent shot in the Library of Congress as "Woodstein" (as they were dubbed) pore over index cards looking for a name. They sit at a desk, surrounded by thousands of cards as the camera moves up, higher and higher, until they look like two tiny men fighting a massive system that has the power to squash them like bugs.

They finally get a break when a political insider, dubbed "Deep Throat," begins to feed them enough information to set them on the right path. Years after the resignation of Nixon, Deep Throat came forward: his name was Mark Felt, compelled to assist the reporters because he was appalled by what Nixon was doing.

Pakula put together an ensemble for the film, and each actor served the screenplay perfectly. It was a credit to William Goldman's work that audiences could make sense of the entire investigation. He gave the film an urgency that captivated us despite the volume of political information.

Rave reviews greeted the film upon release: it was nominated for eight Academy Awards, including Best Picture and Best Director (Pakula), and won for Adapted Screenplay, Art Direction, Best Sound, and Best Supporting Actor for Robards. The New York Film Critics honoured the film with their Best Picture, Best Director, and Best Supporting Actor (Robards), and the National Society of Film Critics named the film Best Picture of the Year. In addition, Pakula was nominated by the Directors Guild of America as Best Director.

Though the film lost the Academy Awards for Best Picture and Best Director, it was the year's finest film and remains as vital and outstanding as it was upon release. It remains a startling historical exploration of the early 70s. Time, often the enemy of a great movie, has had no impact on the picture whatsoever. A superb, literate, entertaining film, *All the President's Men* remains a masterpiece.

Opposite Hoffman and Redford were an inspired choice of casting as the two journalists who brought down Nixon.

130

"*Face to Face* is arguably one of the great films about emotional turmoil, allowing us to witness close-up a woman as she loses her grip on reality during a mental breakdown."

FACE TO FACE (1976)

DIRECTED BY Ingmar Bergman
COUNTRY Sweden

Liv Ullmann was considered one of the greatest actresses in the world before she made *Face to Face* with her former lover Ingmar Bergman. The actress had long been his muse, and their collaborations had produced some of Sweden's finest films. Over the 70s, they created *Cries and Whispers* (1972), *Scenes from a Marriage* (1974), and after *Face to Face*, the extraordinary *Autumn Sonata* (1978), pairing Ullmann with the great Ingrid Bergman.

Ullmann had been an Oscar nominee for her performance in *The Emigrants* (1972) and would be nominated for Best Actress again for her brilliant, shattering performance in *Face to Face*. In addition, she swept the major critics awards, winning Best Actress from the Los Angeles Film Critics Association, the National Board of Review, and the New York Film Critics Circle. She lost the Academy Award to Faye Dunaway in *Network* (1976), a popular choice. In 2022, the Academy of Motion Picture Arts and Sciences awarded Ullmann an Academy Honorary Award for her work as an actress and director and as a UN ambassador for women around the globe.

Face to Face is arguably one of the great films about emotional turmoil, allowing us to witness close-up a woman as she loses her grip on reality during a mental breakdown.

Ullmann is Dr. Jenny Isaksson, a psychiatrist who is temporarily filling in at a local hospital while her daughter is away at summer camp and her husband is in America on business. While selling their home, she moves in with her grandparents, where one room brings on intense feelings of anxiety she fails to understand.

The anxiety is compounded by a near rape at the hands of two men who break into the home. The attack drives Jenny over the edge, and she delves into her past to find answers, but not before suffering a harrowing breakdown. Is she recovered at the end of the film? Does anyone ever heal from such emotional and mental trauma?

Ullmann is almost translucent as Jenny; we can see directly into her soul, where more mystery awaits us. No easy answers to end the movie, just a stunning portrait of a woman going through something terrible that is torturing her. Her performance is regarded as one of the greatest in cinema history and the height of Ullmann's career.

Like all of Bergman's films, *Face to Face* is often chilly and remote, though Ullmann does her best to pull the audience to her. Theirs was one of the most extraordinary actor-director relationships, producing countless brilliant performances.

Opposite Liv Ullmann and her director Ingmar Bergman.

132 KING KONG (1976)

DIRECTED BY John Guillermin
COUNTRY USA

Opposite Jessica Lange was outstanding in this remake of the classic, and went on to be a two-time Oscar-winning actress.

Everything about the 1976 remake of *King Kong* was BIG.

"My monkey is going to be huge," said producer Dino De Laurentiis, and indeed the film was monumental, and the advertising campaign was massive, but the film?

Very little about the film was impressive, but it was as big as they could make it. Peter Jackson's remake twenty-nine years later did everything right, creating a work of art that surpassed the original in beauty, emotion, scope, and visual effects. The 1976 film, though popular with audiences, offered little in comparison.

If there was a saving grace in the film, it was Jessica Lange as the damsel in distress, Dwan. As soon as Kong looks at this blonde beauty, he is smitten, and his fate sealed. Lange must deliver some dreadful lines, but she does her best and gives the film some striking originality. Once in Kong's hands, realizing he might chew her up, she hammers his nose and screams at him, "You goddam chauvinist pig ape, you want to eat me, well EAT ME." The scene drew laughs the three times I saw the film, and it still makes me smile.

Dino De Laurentiis claimed to be creating a love story in which audiences would fall in love with his monkey, but nothing of the kind happened. The problem was that Kong was obviously a man in an ape suit working with miniatures for the action shots. Many of the scenes with Jessica Lange included a mechanical hand. The mechanical giant ape rarely appears and looks fake, stiff, and clumsy, an embarrassment of visual effects.

They arrive on the island hoping to solve the energy crisis in America but instead find an island teeming with unidentified species and a giant ape who takes a shine to the beautiful blonde the men have rescued on their way to the island. The natives kidnap Dwan, drug her, and try to sacrifice her to Kong, a massive ape who storms out of the jungle, knocking over trees, only his eyes visible until finally, we see all twenty-five feet of him.

From there, the story follows the original back to New York, where Kong breaks free and takes Dwan to the top of the World Trade Center (go bigger!), where military helicopters (not the jets of the poster) wage war on the giant ape high above the city. The final battle looks anything but realistic.

Should a film like *King Kong* (1933) even be remade? This 1976 version is updated to the present, losing much of the innocence of the original. Peter Jackson's 2005 version is a sensational film because it pays homage to the original, wisely leaving the film set during the Depression. De Laurentiis did not make the film with love, as Jackson did; he just wanted a blockbuster that would make money.

Jessica Lange broke out in the 1976 remake. Three years later, she was superb as the Angel of Death in Bob Fosse's *All That Jazz* (1979); three years after that, she won an Oscar for Best Supporting Actress in *Tootsie* (1982) and a nomination for Best Actress in *Frances* (1982). Not once does she look ridiculous during *King Kong*, which is far more than we can say for the giant ape.

Guillermin gives the film an epic sweep, bolstered by a beautiful score, but the weak production is too much to overcome. The snake he fights in the cave looks particularly fake, and that waterfall scene where the great ape washes Dwan off while making goo-goo eyes at her? The groans gradually became howls of laughter... enough said.

"Very little about the film was impressive, but it was as big as they could make it."

"Szell is among the most frightful villains to ever appear in a movie. Often overrated, Olivier lives up to his name with this performance."

MARATHON MAN (1976)

DIRECTED BY John Schlesinger
COUNTRY USA

Academy Award-winning screenwriter William Goldman adapted his thriller novel *Marathon Man* for the screenplay of this terrifying film, one of the darkest of the decade.

To fully appreciate the film, you must realize from the beginning that Babe Levy (Dustin Hoffman) is innocent and has no idea what his brother does. Nor does he know why these people are suddenly in his life, meaning him harm. Babe is a brilliant history major hoping to clear his father's name from accusations that he was a communist sympathizer brought forth during the McCarthy hearings. His brother Doc (Roy Scheider) is a government agent offering courier services to Christian Szell (Laurence Olivier), a Nazi dentist now living in Paraguay, in return for his assistance in finding war criminals. When Szell is forced to come to America, he wants to go to the diamond market to sell his cache of diamonds but fears he may be robbed. He kills Doc thinking he intends to steal the diamonds, leading Szell directly to Babe.

Szell has Babe brought to an abandoned warehouse, where he tortures him, asking him the same question over and over, "Is it safe?" As he asks, he is examining Babe's teeth. Finding a cavity, he suddenly and violently rams a probe directly into the exposed nerve. The pain is excruciating. Of course, Babe tells him nothing because he knows nothing. Later, believing Babe is holding out, Szell brings him back and this time, drills into a live nerve. Babe somehow escapes and being a marathon runner, bolts from the street to his home.

By now, he knows he can trust no one, especially when he learns the girl he has been seeing belongs to Szell. When Szell goes to the diamond market, an elderly Jewish woman recognizes him as the monster she knew from the death camps, the White Angel. Finally, face to face with a walking, living, deplorable piece of history, Babe kills Szell, throws his gun into the water, and walks away.

The performances in the film are uniformly superb, but Hoffman and Olivier are standouts. Szell is among the most frightful villains to ever appear in a movie. Often overrated, Olivier lives up to his name with this performance. The sequence in the diamond market where he is recognized is startling because of his absolute confidence in killing the man who recognizes him. No hesitation, just a flick of the hand holding the blade, and one sweep cuts the startled man's throat.

Schlesinger gives the film an unbearable tension, and the twists and turns keep the audience guessing. Learning Janeway (William Devane) is with Szell was a stunner! Superbly directed and edited, the film was a hit with audience and critics, and the dentist business probably took a severe blow.

Opposite In this John Schlesinger thriller, Dustin Hoffman plays a young historian who comes face to face with a vicious Nazi from the past.

136 NETWORK (1976)

DIRECTED BY Sidney Lumet
COUNTRY USA

Opposite Behind the scenes at a major network, ambitious, dangerous Diana (Faye Dunaway) oversees the network news.

Sitting in a board room, a group of television executives debates how to deal with the troublesome though beloved Howard Beale, once the news anchor, now a TV star. Grimly, one of them suggests, "Well, I guess we're going to have to kill him." No one laughs, and no one protests. They proceed to choose their assassin and carry it out on live television. As they hoped, it gets "a hell of a rating."

Network is a lacerating, satiric black comedy that foreshadows the explosion of reality television thirty years before it began. It portrays the toxic personalities who work in the competitive, unforgiving world of network television, where you are only as good as your latest hit. Written by two-time Academy Award winner Paddy Chayevsky who worked in television for many years, and directed by Sidney Lumet, who in recent years seemed to be guiding actors to Oscar nominations and wins, *Network* proved no exception to that claim, as five of its cast were Academy Award nominees, three of them winners.

After Howard Beale (Peter Finch) has a breakdown on network television while reporting the news, UBS (a fictional network) allows him back on to say goodbye to his loyal viewers. Beale uses the opportunity to rant about being sick of all the "bullshit" in life. Rather than seek help for this man in the throes of a breakdown, the network chief fires the news director Max (William Holden) and promotes the ambitious and scheming Diana (Faye Dunaway), who smells a hit.

A few nights later, Beale enters the newsroom from a driving rainstorm. He goes on air, looking like a wet rat. There, as if possessed, he orders the viewers to get mad, to go to their windows, throw them open, and scream, "I'm as mad as hell, and I'm not going to take it anymore!" So fired up, Beale finishes and collapses on live television. In an instant, Howard Beale is the biggest thing on TV, and lowly UBS, consistently in fourth place, has the top-rated show on television.

Beale slowly breaks from reality, believing that God is speaking to him. Why him? God explains, "Because you're on television, dummy." Meanwhile, Max and Diana have an affair, his marriage ends, and Howard continues his tirades. However, when he takes on the television network on air, the owner of the network calls him in. Jensen persuades him to change his message to support the network. Howard asks why he must be the messenger, and Jensen answers, "Because you're on television, dummy." Howard responds that he has seen the face of God, to which Jensen replies, "You just might be right, Mr. Beale."

But Howard does not follow through. He gets worse and ruins a massive deal of Jensen's, leading us into the board room where they decide to have him killed on live television. They do just that, and television, they tell us, carried relentlessly on.

Network is a stunning film. The performances are superb, beginning with Dunaway's cold, calculating Diana, who cannot talk about anything, even during sex, other than television. And when Max ends it with her, he predicts she will one day take a flying leap out of an office window to the cement below, ending her misery.

Holden, no longer the strikingly good-looking leading man he was in the 50s, is superb as craggy, defeated Max, who is looking for something to believe in and wrongly believes it is Diana. We can only hope his wounded wife, magnificently portrayed by Beatrice Straight, will take him back. Robert Duvall is arrogant and smug as Frank Hackett, the head of the network for Mr. Jensen, portrayed with bluster and fury by Ned Beatty in a startling seven-minute sequence.

And Peter Finch as Beale, a superb supporting performance that the Academy believed was a lead for some reason. Looking like a broken old lion, Finch seems bewildered by life. It is a sensational performance from an actor they did not initially want (Jack Lemmon was their first choice).

"*Network* is a lacerating, satiric black comedy that foreshadows the explosion of reality television thirty years before it began."

Nominated for ten Academy Awards, including five of its actors, Finch and Holden for Best Actor, Dunaway for Best Actress, and Beatty and Straight for Supporting Actor and Actress. In addition, *Network* was up for Best Picture, Best Director, and Best Original Screenplay. It would win four Oscars in all, for Finch (posthumously), Dunaway, Straight, and Chayevsky would collect a third award for writing. Lumet was a Directors Guild nominee and earned some of the finest reviews of his career.

Though Finch was excellent, many struggled with his win for Best Actor for what was clearly a supporting role. The Academy's choice also meant Robert De Niro, who was searing in *Taxi Driver*, would go home empty-handed.

It is one of the most caustic and brilliant black comedies ever made, perhaps because it is all so plausible. And that made it terrifying.

INTERMISSION: THE BEACH HOUSE GANG MAKES GOOD

If you were to arrive in Malibu in the late 60s at the rented beach house of actresses Margot Kidder and Jennifer Salt, years away from their big break in movies, you might encounter the following scene.

Holding court, as was his habit, likely seated in the middle of the room, talking loudly, gesturing wildly, was Francis Ford Coppola. The self-appointed leader had made some films already, including a studio film, but had yet to find great success. At his side, always, was his student, George Lucas, a quiet, unassuming young man with a fertile imagination and totally in awe of Coppola. Coppola mostly discussed how he wanted to become independent of the studios, never needing their money to make a film. Lucas heartily agreed.

Outdoors, swimming or surfing, was writer John Milius, who never found the success the others did as a director but was very much part of the early gang.

Brian De Palma, the ladies' man of the group, tried his best to seduce any new woman who might find her way to the beach house.

In the corner, just listening, was Steven Spielberg. The painfully shy Spielberg did not share Coppola's opinion of being independent of the studio and was already on Universal's radar as an up-and-coming talent.

A knock on the door announced the arrival of diminutive Martin Scorsese, dressed immaculately in a three-piece white suit, complete with a coloured tie on a summer's day. He carried flowers for their hosts, Kidder and Salt, and greeted his friends warmly, talking in machine gun, rat-a-tat delivery.

The conversation was about cinema. The films they loved, the films they hated, and the films they wanted to make. Each one was gifted and would go on to great success, but for now, they were dreamers about to alter the course of film. Hollywood had changed dramatically through the 60s, as though it were preparing itself for these men and the stories they wanted to tell. The older, established directors were retiring or dying off, and the studio system was nearly dead, so the time for new emerging talents had arrived.

For now, they had these gatherings, the chili cooked by Kidder and Salt, conversations with good friends, and their dreams. How did they find one another? How did they come together? In the coming decade, each would enjoy either box office or critical success, or both for the lucky ones.

Years later, in 2007, Coppola, Lucas, and Spielberg would stand on a stage and present Scorsese with a long overdue Academy Award for Best Director. After five nominations for Best Director, Scorsese finally won his award. He has earned three more nominations since. By 2007, Coppola had won five Oscars: one for producing, one for directing (with four other nominations), and three for writing. Spielberg had three: one for producing and two for directing

Right George Lucas on-set with his young stars.

Below The young up-and-comers, now the old guard, presenting Martin Scorsese with a long overdue Academy Award for Best Director.

"The conversation was about cinema. The films they loved, the films they hated, and the films they wanted to make."

(with seven other nominations). Lucas had won an Honorary Oscar and been twice nominated for Best Director. Collectively, the quartet represents twenty-four Academy Award nominations for Best Director.

They were now the old guard of Hollywood and a long way from that small beach house.

140 ROCKY (1976)

DIRECTED BY John G. Avildsen
COUNTRY USA

Opposite Under the watchful eye of Mickey (Burgess Meredith), Rocky (Sylvester Stallone) trains for the heavyweight championship of the world. The narrative in the film mirrored the story of Stallone, himself a million to one shot.

The story behind how *Rocky* came to the screen could be a movie. Except, audiences would say the story was too hard to believe, too Hollywood.

Sylvester Stallone was a bit part actor. The roles were not there for him anymore, and he was getting squeezed out of Hollywood. Married, with a child on the way, he struggled to support his family. Inspired by the Ali–Wepner fight on television, he began to write and completed the screenplay to *Rocky* in three and a half days. That was the easy part; the challenge was convincing Hollywood studios that he should play the part of Rocky. Everyone loved the script, but no one wanted his casting idea. They made offers to buy it for Ryan O'Neal, James Caan, even Burt Reynolds, but Stallone held firm, declining offers of over $150,000. Back then, that was enough to provide an adequate nest egg for his family. But he knew playing the role would alter the course of his life, and he wasn't compromising.

United Artists agreed to give him the lead role and to choreograph the boxing sequences. The only catch was the offer came with a $1 million budget—bare bones. Journeyman director John G. Avildsen directed the film, with actors Talia Shire (Adrian), Burgess Meredith (Mickey), Burt Young (Paulie), and Carl Weathers (Apollo Creed)—mostly veteran character actors, but no stars.

The shoot was a mere twenty-eight days in and around Philadelphia.

When the film premiered in the fall of 1976, it was lightning in a bottle. No one expected this kind of brilliance, this kind of art. It was like the British kitchen sink dramas of the early 60s, down and dirty. Organizers want a gimmick fight on New Year's Eve with the heavyweight champion of the world, Apollo Creed, obviously modelled on Muhammad Ali. Rocky, a local club fighter, is chosen not for his talent but his nickname, "The Italian Stallion." He accepts the challenge, hoping to prove to himself and others that he is not "just another bum from the neighbourhood."

Rocky chooses Mickey (Burgess Meredith) as his trainer, a cantankerous old man who never got his chance. Despite dismissing Rocky as a "tomato," Mickey begs him to let him train. The two make amends, and Mickey is soon training Rocky to take on the best fighter in the world. We see a montage of Rocky devoting himself to training while Apollo lounges, taking care of press work.

The fight sequence is breathtaking, intense, electrifying, and violent. It literally drew people to their feet. Never in my life had I watched a movie audience respond to a film like this. It was like they were watching a live sporting event with their favourite team. Rocky does not win, but he does go the full fifteen rounds with Apollo, which no one had ever done before. The film closes with Rocky and Adrian embracing and declaring their love.

What continues to be shocking about the film is that it avoids cliche. No David and Goliath here. Rocky does not win the fight. He gives and gets a terrible beating, but he does not win.

The film was a massive hit at the box office and nominated for ten Academy Awards, including Best Picture, Best Director, Best Actor (Stallone), Best Actress (Shire), and two nominees for Best Supporting Actor (Meredith and Young). Stallone became the first man in thirty-five years to be nominated for both actor and screenplay, not to mention an overnight superstar. He was not, however, the next coming of Brando, as many writers predicted. Not even close.

“No one expected this kind of brilliance, this kind of art. It was like the British kitchen sink dramas of the early 60s, down and dirty.”

"This was her zenith, her career's highest moment, never to be achieved again."

SEVEN BEAUTIES (1976)

DIRECTED BY Lina Wertmüller
COUNTRY Italy

Seven Beauties received an Oscar nomination for Best Director, marking a precedent for the Academy because the director in this case was a woman. They could argue that there were very few women to choose from up to that point, although female directors were commonplace on stage. Wertmüller had enjoyed growing popularity with her films over the previous five years, especially *Swept Away* (1975), but the reception that greeted *Seven Beauties* was extraordinary. Hailed by film critics across North America as a stinging work of art, the film was on countless top ten lists by the end of the year, and then came the announcement of the Academy Award nominations.

In addition to Best Director, a massive coup for the film, *Seven Beauties* was nominated for Best Actor (Giancarlo Giannini for his triumphant performance), Best Original Screenplay (Wertmüller again), and Best Foreign Language Film, the Oscar it was most likely to win.

It is a dark story set during WWII, about a man, Pasqualino (Giannini), who kills a man and packs his body parts into suitcases after an outrageous insult to his family. Caught by the police, he goes to jail but lands in a German concentration camp in a curious turn of events.

Trying to stay alive with painful desperation, he attempts to seduce the monstrous Commandant of the camp, a hideous woman who enjoys the suffering she inflicts on the prisoners in her charge. When Pasqualino professes his love, she makes him prove it by making love to her, and while he manages to perform, she is underwhelmed. In a perverse and cruel move, she places him in charge of deciding which men will die, forcing him to choose his friend.

He makes it home only to discover to his horror that his sister and mother have become prostitutes as a matter of survival. After killing a man to defend the honour of his sister, he realizes the irony of it all, as the memories sweep over his haunted face.

The sad, mournful eyes of Giancarlo Giannini might have been his greatest asset as an actor. He captures truth in every moment he is on the screen. He had shone brightly in *Swept Away* one year before, but *Seven Beauties* remains his most extraordinary screen performance, a stunning achievement that richly deserved the Oscar nomination he received.

American actress Shirley Stoler was superb as the vile Commandant, though she never did much after this performance.

And Wertmüller?

This was her zenith, the high point of her career, never to be achieved again. But this spectacular masterpiece gave hope and inspiration to all the female directors who followed her. Jane Campion, Sofia Coppola, Sarah Polley, Penny Marshall, and so many others owe her a debt.

Opposite Sad-eyed Giancarlo Giannini was superb in this Italian masterpiece, earning an Oscar nomination for Best Actor.

144 TAXI DRIVER (1976)

DIRECTED BY Martin Scorsese
COUNTRY USA

Opposite His volcanic fury barely contained, Travis (Robert De Niro) begins the process of training for his self-imposed mission to clean up the filth in New York. De Niro seethes throughout this frightening film directed by Martin Scorsese.

Back in 1976, you might have thought the steam billowing out of the maintenance-hole covers on the streets of New York was coming directly from hell. Light years from the Disneyland it is today, Times Square was once a scary place to visit, full of hookers, massage parlours, thieves, drug dealers, and the dregs of humanity. When Travis Bickle (Robert De Niro) refers to it as an "open sewer," he is not wrong.

Taxi Driver opened to rave reviews and shocked audiences. The movie announced the emergence of new talent—director Martin Scorsese, actor Robert De Niro—and one of the darkest films ever made. Like Stanley Kubrick, Scorsese demands that you experience, rather than watch, his pictures.

Travis is a Vietnam veteran with insomnia; he uses it to his advantage when he takes a job as a New York cabbie, willing to drive in the wee hours of the morning and go anywhere in the city. He becomes dangerously obsessive about cleaning up the city and the streets. The only bright spot in his life is Betsy (Cybill Shepherd), a pretty young woman working in a political campaign office. They date very briefly, ending when Travis takes her to a hardcore porn film, which disgusts her. Travis truly cannot understand his mistake and is devastated.

His array of clientele—child prostitutes, pimps, drug dealers, jilted husbands—pushes Travis over the edge. He begins to get back into shape, buys an arsenal of guns, and plans his attacks.

When his assassination attempt on the candidate Betsy was working for fails, he goes after a pimp named Sport (Harvey Keitel) and the men working for him. He plans to free Iris (Jodie Foster), a twelve-year-old hooker working for them. Though he plans to save her from the evils of New York, he also chooses to have her witness a full blood bath first.

The killing sequence was among the most violent movie-goers had ever seen. Intensely realistic, the blood flows copiously.

Where to start with De Niro? He is, throughout the film, a time bomb ticking away. We know he is planning a slaughter, but we don't know his target. Had he successfully assassinated Palantine, would Betsy have been next? Was Travis's plan always to kill himself once he finished? Ironically, Travis is elevated to the status of hero for "rescuing" Iris and returning her home. After his recovery, we search for proof his sanity has returned as he delivers Betsy in his cab without incident. Yet we catch his eyes in the rearview mirror and once again, see a crazed man.

De Niro was no less than astonishing as Travis Bickle. He radiates danger each time he comes into frame, as his eyes land on a character, sizing them up, deciding if they are worthy of living. Equally remarkable is Jodie Foster as the young Iris, a bold and daring performance from the very young actress. As Sport, her pimp, Harvey Keitel is all jittery nerves and motion until crossed, when he becomes aggressive and violent.

Scorsese creates a New York with shocking realism and an intense documentary-like feel that enhances the film, making it all the more frightening.

It was nominated for four Academy Awards, including Best Picture, Best Actor (De Niro), and Best Supporting Actress (Foster), and won both the National Society of Film Critics Award and the New York York Film Critics Award for Best Actor.

Darkly stunning.

“Like Stanley Kubrick, Scorsese demands that you experience, rather than watch, his pictures.”

"Despite all the talent, United Artists quickly realized they had a problem upon release. Critics did not care for the film, and audiences stayed away."

THE MISSOURI BREAKS (1976)

DIRECTED BY Arthur Penn
COUNTRY USA

Of the four American westerns made in 1976, three of which are explored in this book, *The Missouri Breaks* was the most anticipated and then the most criticized. It has grown in stature through the years but far too often is described as a weak film because of the performance of Marlon Brando. Was it ruined because of Marlon Brando?

Not at all.

The haunting final scene will stay with you long after—Tom Logan (Nicholson) standing over Robert Lee Clayton (Brando), waking him in the middle of the night with an ominous single line. "You know what woke you? You just had your throat cut," he tells Clayton, watching as a trickle of blood falls out of his victim's mouth. It would be a gruesome way to go, even by the standards of the Old West, even by the standards of Clayton, a hired assassin who manages to find creative ways to kill his targets. Clayton always avoids looking into his victim's eyes, choosing to kill from afar, which might be why Logan kills him in the manner he does, forcing him to look at him. The scene is intimate and deeply personal, beautifully acted by two masters, and expertly directed.

The Missouri Breaks was the only film in which Marlon Brando and Jack Nicholson co-starred and thus was considered a major motion picture event. The two acclaimed actors were also excited about the prospect of working together. They knew they were in good hands with director Arthur Penn, and together they created a revisionist western, something new and unique. Despite all the talent, United Artists quickly realized they had a problem upon release. Critics did not care for the film, and audiences stayed away. Brando's performance took most of the shots, with critics mocking his accents, his disguises, and generally everything he did in the film. Did they forget he was portraying an unbalanced character? It was a strange reaction to such a flawless actor.

"Aim the camera, light him, and let him go," a director once said of Brando, "he will give you magic."

The Missouri Breaks was unlike any western ever seen, an original. Many critics, myself included, found the film original and wildly inventive. Brando took brave risks with his character, but was it over the top? He was consistently bizarre but what he did on screen worked for the character, always believable. Logan was the steadier of the two, an outlaw trying to go straight and quietly work his modest farm. Tired of being on the run, tired of seeing his friends die, he believes he might make a life with the daughter of the very man hunting him down.

The two great actors do not share many scenes, but the screen crackles with energy and intensity when they are together. The finest occurs as Brando bathes in a bubble bath as Nicholson rages above him. It is the only scene where Brando is not self-indulgent in his acting, where he gives to the other actor rather than takes.

The cinematography depicts an Old West as it must have been: violent, dirty, vast, and isolated. No question, life was hard, but some people managed to eke out an existence. Others like Tom Logan sought the quicker route to success by stealing.

The entire promotional campaign for this movie focused on the star actors. No question, it was exciting settling into your cinema seat, knowing you were about to see at least two great performances. Not everything about the picture works, but Brando's choices were endlessly fascinating and often wildly original. Kathleen Lloyd made an impressive debut, but her career never took off.

The Missouri Breaks has moments of brilliance but doesn't manage to maintain it for the entire length of the film.

Opposite Two generations of great actors, Brando and Nicholson are pitted against one another in this revisionist western.

"Wayne has autumnal chemistry with Lauren Bacall that is entirely unexpected but wonderful to watch, and young Ron Howard is outstanding."

THE SHOOTIST (1976)

DIRECTED BY Don Siegel
COUNTRY USA

Paramount Pictures dropped the ball badly when they decided to release *The Shootist* in the summer amidst the blockbusters. It should have been an awards season release between September and December. Finding a cinema that was showing the film in the summer of 76 was a challenge.

Audiences underestimated John Wayne as an actor, accusing him of simply playing himself. But when matched with a strong director like John Ford or Howard Hawks, Wayne was an excellent actor. He knew his limitations and never tried to overreach. He could never do Shakespeare any more than Laurence Olivier or John Gielgud could appear in a western. Wayne was at home in westerns, war films, and pretty much anything directed by John Ford. Ford discovered Wayne's talent after seeing *Red River* (1948), announcing, "I never knew the son of a bitch could act!" He began casting Wayne in major films, and Wayne returned the favour with brilliant performances, repeatedly proving that Ford was right. His roles in *She Wore a Yellow Ribbon* (1949), *The Quiet Man* (1952), and most of all, his seething, towering work in *The Searchers* (1956) should have earned him Academy Award nominations and the Oscar itself for *The Searchers*. He would finally win for *True Grit* (1969), a sentimental award for lifetime achievement. The Academy had one more chance to honour the actor, and they chose not to do so.

The movie was *The Shootist*. As J. B. Books, he is a legend in the West, arriving in town in 1901 on the day Queen Victoria died. Books has advanced cancer, which will soon bring the kind of pain no human should ever endure. He is in town to see a doctor he trusts to get a second opinion on his diagnosis. With nowhere to go and no family or loved ones, he decides to stay in the town to die, but he won't go gently.

"I'm a dying man afraid of the dark," he tells his landlady, Mrs. Rogers, played by the lovely Lauren Bacall. In another time, he and Mrs. Rogers might have been a couple. Though they become friends, their time together is short-lived. With the help of Mrs. Rogers's son Gillom (Ron Howard), Books challenges three of the best shots in town to a duel to the death. Being still lightning fast and knowing his way around a gunfight, he kills all three but is shot in the back by the cowardly bartender. Gillom then kills the bartender before throwing the gun away, not wanting the life Books led.

Wayne is superb in the film, vulnerable, haunted, and finally haunting. He has autumnal chemistry with Lauren Bacall that is entirely unexpected but wonderful to watch, and young Ron Howard is outstanding.

One of the last great American westerns before the genre died with *Heaven's Gate* (1980), *The Shootist* was a fitting epitaph to Wayne, though an Oscar nomination would have made it a perfect Hollywood ending. Still, it was a great tribute to a legend—and one of Wayne's best performances.

Opposite John Wayne's final film, a melancholy story of a former gunfighter dying of cancer and seeking peace before his death Wayne, Lauren Bacall, James Stewart, and Ron Howard were superb.

150 ANNIE HALL (1977)

DIRECTED BY Woody Allen
COUNTRY USA

Opposite Breaking the rules for romantic comedy, *Annie Hall* had no happy ending, Annie (Diane Keaton) having outgrown Alvy (Allen). Beautifully acted, directed, and written, the film announced Woody Allen as a major new filmmaker.

Hollywood romantic comedies had followed a formulaic plot for more than forty years: boy meets girl, boy loses girl, boy gets girl back. The happy ending was mandatory—the couple had to be together by the time the credits rolled.

In 1977, filmmaker Woody Allen revolutionized the genre by adding a new twist that made the genre vastly more realistic: boy loses girl forever. Perhaps they have outgrown one another, work better as friends, or realize they are better off alone. Whatever the reason, by the end of *Annie Hall*, the couple we have been watching for two hours has de-coupled.

The movie is loosely based on Allen's relationship with actress Diane Keaton. After writing the screenplay, he dared to ask her to play the role in the film opposite himself. Bold, an act of genius.

With *Annie Hall*, Allen leaped into the forefront of American filmmakers. In the years since, he has averaged a film a year, sometimes two, earned rave reviews, won Academy Awards and critics' awards, weathered a scandal that might have ruined lesser men, and given us some of the finest screen comedies of the last fifty years. *Annie Hall*, his masterpiece *Manhattan* (1979), the vastly underrated *Stardust Memories* (1980), *Broadway Danny Rose* (1984), *The Purple Rose of Cairo* (1985), *Hannah and Her Sisters* (1986), *Crimes and Misdemeanors* (1989), *Bullets Over Broadway* (1994), *Vicky Cristina Barcelona* (2008), and the breathtaking *Midnight in Paris* (2011) are his finest works, with the murder mystery *Match Point* (2005) joining them as soaring works of art.

In *Annie Hall*, Allen and Keaton portray Alvy and Annie, two New Yorkers who meet, fall in love, move in together, break up, get back together, and then end their relationship forever. Allen tells the story with striking purity and honesty. Most of us will inevitably recognize our own lives throughout the movie, especially the breakup and reconciliation scenes and the slow disintegration of their relationship. It is so natural and organic and certainly nobody's fault. The breakup gives the film a sadness, a bittersweet conclusion that Hollywood love stories never had. It was breathtaking to watch such honesty.

Beautifully exploring scenes from his life, his memories growing up in Brooklyn, his first sexual encounter, the evolution of their relationship from romantic beginnings to the shocking realization she is straying, and the pain of losing her are all played out with humour and realism in every frame. That they remain friends, as Allen and Keaton have, makes perfect sense because how could one who meant so much walk out of your life?

Keaton was a revelation as Annie, breaking into the ranks of leading actresses with her performance, winning all the prominent critics' awards and the Academy Award. Despite being up against *Star Wars* (1977), *Annie Hall* was nominated for five Academy Awards and won Best Picture, Best Actress, Best Director, and Best Screenplay. Allen also received his only nomination for Best Actor thus far.

Christopher Walken has a cameo role as Annie's nutty brother who admits to fantasizing about steering his car into oncoming traffic just before he drives Alvy and Annie to the airport.

In the canon of Woody Allen films, *Annie Hall* has remained at or near the top of the long list of his impressive work. Even though he remains outside the Hollywood system, being a die-hard New Yorker, he might be the finest screenwriter in Hollywood history. Though he famously skips the Academy Awards events, he attended after 9/11 to introduce a tribute to New York. That city might be the real love of his life.

"In the canon of Woody Allen films, *Annie Hall* has remained at or near the top of the long list of his impressive work."

"Bruce Dern is terrifying and yet vulnerable as Michael, a broken and dangerous man."

BLACK SUNDAY (1977)

DIRECTED BY John Frankenheimer
COUNTRY USA

Like everyone else in North America, I was glued to my television on September 11, 2001, watching the endless replays of the two planes that crashed into the World Trade Center, an attack by terrorists on America. I could not believe the sheer destruction, the gaping hole where the towers once loomed over the New York skyline. The area around the towers looking like a war zone. New Yorkers wandered through the suddenly empty streets in a state of shock, trying to fathom a hatred as deep as this. How does one explain that kind of hatred to their children?

In 1977, John Frankenheimer brought *Black Sunday* to the screen, a dark thriller about terrorism based on a best-selling book by Thomas Harris, who would later write *The Silence of the Lambs*. Paramount Pictures bought the rights to *Black Sunday* and created a film they felt would be a blockbuster, a massive hit that would score at the box office.

Despite being dropped by cinemas within three weeks, the film is brilliant and remains the best of the genre dealing with international terrorism. Deeply unsettling, the movie tapped into a genuine fear and exploited that terror throughout.

A terrorist group, "Black September," plans to detonate a bomb containing thousands of deadly darts in the stadium during the annual Super Bowl game, killing everyone, including the President of the United States, who is scheduled to attend the game. They have recruited a former American prisoner of war from Vietnam to help with their cause. Michael J. Lander (Bruce Dern) is a pilot who flies the Goodyear Blimp during the football games for the television networks. Fearless, he is also psychotic. After years of torture as a POW in the Vietnam War, Lander wants revenge on the country that betrayed him, the people he feels abandoned him. The Black September movement convinces him this is his chance, sending the beautiful operative Dahlia (Marthe Keller) to seduce and persuade him to go along with their attack. Using the Goodyear Blimp, they will detonate a bomb. Lander has built the device, tested it, and knows the destruction will be complete.

The Israeli secret police come to America after finding a video tape on which a woman's voice can be heard discussing an attack on American soil. Kabakov (Robert Shaw) had encountered Dahlia during a raid on the terrorists' headquarters and had a chance to kill her but let her go. Now, working with the American FBI and CIA, the Israelis hope to find Dahlia and prevent the attack.

The film is an intense thriller from the moment it opens in Beirut. It has all the makings of a blockbuster, but it never had a chance since it was released in the summer when audiences were seeing *Star Wars* (1977) for the tenth time. Too bad because *Black Sunday* is an electrifying piece of work.

Bruce Dern is terrifying and yet vulnerable as Michael, a man who dedicated himself to the military only to lose everything. He is a broken and dangerous man. His breakdown describing what happened when he came home from the war is astonishing in its visceral power. It is a superb performance that richly deserved to be among the Academy Award nominees of 1977. His performance was more potent than all five nominees for Best Actor.

Marthe Keller is excellent as Dahlia, the only person who seems able to control Michael, as is Robert Shaw as the Israeli agent who loses a dear friend to the terrorists as he works to uncover their plot.

Though the cinema is not real life, watching the planes crash into the towers in New York brought back the terror I felt watching the Goodyear Blimp crashing into the stadium. One can never understand or even fathom a hatred this deep.

Opposite Two deadly terrorists finalize their plot to blow up the Super Bowl. Lander (Bruce Dern) teaches Dahlia (Marthe Keller) the names of the Goodyear Blimp pilots and crew. Dern was devastating as Lander, both dangerous and vulnerable.

154

CLOSE ENCOUNTERS OF THE THIRD KIND (1977)

DIRECTED BY Steven Spielberg
COUNTRY USA

Opposite Contact. A child is drawn to the wonder of an alien ship landing in his front yard. Miraculous.

"It was like seeing God," I overheard a woman say as we exited the cinema moments after seeing Steven Spielberg's dreamscape. It was a common reaction to this extraordinary film about man's first contact with aliens. Nothing hostile—they are not here to mine our planet or render humanity extinct. They want only to let us know they have been around a while and to return some of the people and items they had borrowed through the years.

Spielberg's final forty-five minutes held his audiences in awe and rapture.

A group of scientists investigate how aeroplanes that vanished during the Second World War have now been discovered in a desert, looking as pristine as when they disappeared. Meanwhile, a massive cargo ship appears in the desert, along with various reported sightings of UFOs, including a man who explains that the sun came out last night and sang to him. The aliens implant a random group of individuals with a vision inviting them to something incredible. Roy Neary (Richard Dreyfuss) is among the people so implanted, but it takes him a while to solve the mystery. He eventually discovers the mountain in his vision is Devils Tower in Wyoming.

All interested parties head to Wyoming, including scientists and the military, who do not want any witnesses, so they create diversions to scare people away. But Roy and his friend Jillian (Melinda Dillon) manage to get through and scale the mountain. She is looking for her little boy who was taken by the aliens one night.

On the other side of the mountain, they discover a runway. Countless scientists are already there, awaiting the arrival of the aliens, who finally appear in a massive ship more prominent than the mountain. It opens in a blast of white light, and people begin to disembark, people who have vanished through the last hundred years. We learn that the creatures abducted, studied, cared for, and now are returning them. They have not aged a day. And yes, the little boy is among them, safe and sound.

And then the aliens emerge. They are magnificent—white, thin, hairless. And whom do they approach? Roy, the purest of them all. They escort him onto the ship to begin his journey into the stars.

The final moments have the alien leader approach Dr. Lacombe (François Truffaut), head of the search for the aliens, and offer him five signals used in teaching music to the deaf. Lacombe matches them and sends them back, bringing a smile to the face of the creature.

Spielberg made a sensational film about what would be the most significant day in the history of humanity, the confirmation of life beyond earth. It is a work of beauty and poetry that blissfully dazed audiences.

Richard Dreyfuss gives one of his finest performances as the childlike Roy, though many critics struggled with him leaving behind his wife and children. But how could he pass this up? He needed answers to something extraordinary and was going to get them. It was a superb performance from an actor who won the Oscar that year for *The Goodbye Girl*.

Nominated for eight Academy Awards (but incredibly not Best Picture), the film earned two Oscars for Best Cinematography and a Special Award with *Star Wars* for Visual Effects. These two films kicked off a new generation of science fiction that would dominate the landscape for years to come. So many films came along with aliens visiting here to dominate or ruin the earth; very few had the wonder and glory of *Close Encounters of the Third Kind*. It truly was a miracle of a movie.

“It is a work of beauty and poetry that blissfully dazed audiences.”

156 **“Keaton deserved two nominations this year—for *Looking for Mr. Goodbar* and for *Annie Hall*, which won her the Academy Award.”**

LOOKING FOR MR. GOODBAR (1977)

DIRECTED BY Richard Brooks
COUNTRY USA

Looking for Mr. Goodbar was among the darkest films released in the 70s, a startling character study that portrayed complex people who defied categorization or easy judgement. The movie comes from the shocking true story of Roseann Quinn, a teacher who worked with deaf children by day and cruised bars for men by night. She was twenty-seven years old when the man she took home butchered her.

Judith Rossner first captured Quinn's story in a best-selling novel, and Richard Brooks adapted the book into a film he directed and wrote.

Diane Keaton gave the performance of a lifetime in the film as Theresa Dunn, a character with a broader range than we had seen in Hollywood—a Madonna and a tramp, all within minutes of each other. Mistreated by the men she loved in her life, Theresa frequents bars looking for love, or at least affirmation that she is worthy of being loved. Singles bars become her favourite places; she comes nightly with book in hand, focused on finding the right guy. She is not choosy about who she takes home, though we at least understand the thrill of being with the irresistible Tony (Richard Gere).

She finally picks up the wrong guy, a cowboy portrayed superbly by Tom Berenger. Unable to achieve an erection, he suspects she is making fun of him, and he rapes and kills her, stabbing her numerous times in a horrific scene that is hard to forget. In the book, it was terrifying; on film, it is far worse.

Until this movie, Keaton was known for her comedic work for Woody Allen in *Play It Again, Sam* (1972), *Love and Death* (1975), and *Annie Hall* (1977) and as Kay Corleone in *The Godfather* (1972) and *The Godfather Part II* (1974). Keaton deserved two nominations this year—for *Looking for Mr. Goodbar* and for *Annie Hall*, which won her the Academy Award. However, the Academy inexplicably prohibits actors from being nominated twice in one category for two different performances.

Keaton is utterly fearless in the role, portraying a character who could easily come across as dislikable, especially in this era, but never does. With this pair of performances in 1977, she claimed her place as one of America's new great actresses. The array of characters she has portrayed through the years has demonstrated her extraordinary range. Though she has enjoyed a brilliant career, 1977 was the year when she produced her finest work to date.

Tuesday Weld is terrific as Theresa's sexually liberated sister, and Richard Gere is electrifying as her lover Tony, probably his best work as well, bringing incredible energy to each scene.

Richard Brooks delivered an authenticity to the film that is perfect in tone and never steps over the line into sensationalism. Knowing the story rules the day, he allows it to unfold and permits Keaton to take centre stage with her searing performance. While some narrow-minded critics of the time believed the story was a cautionary warning to promiscuous women, many concluded that the story was about a sexually expressive woman who made a wrong choice.

Opposite Diane Keaton demonstrates her astounding range as a promiscuous school teacher, pictured here with Richard Gere in one of his first roles. A dark, cautionary film that ends in tragedy.

158 NEW YORK, NEW YORK (1977)

DIRECTED BY Martin Scorsese
COUNTRY USA

Opposite Though often brave and daring, Scorsese's surrealistic musical is undone by the obnoxious performance of Robert De Niro as a gifted saxophone player. Liza Minnelli is luminous as Francine the young singer on her way up.

Though now restored to how Scorsese intended the narrative, we cannot forget that the studio interfered with the director's final cut of the film, taking out key sequences and destroying the storyline of the film. Granted, the studio had its reasons for being impatient: the budget had nearly tripled; Scorsese's affair with Liza Minnelli did not go unnoticed; and the director's use of cocaine almost killed him. Had he been given free rein, he most certainly would have died. When Robert De Niro finally got him to a hospital, the doctors told the diminutive Scorsese, "You have no platelets."

Imagine modern cinema without Martin Scorsese.

Fresh from the rave reviews and strong box office performance of his seething film *Taxi Driver* (1976), Scorsese was in a position of power. He convinced United Artists to bankroll a musical for him that would be original but also pay homage to the glorious films he watched as a child—*An American in Paris* (1951) and *Singin' in the Rain* (1952) most notably. Though musicals were still being produced, they were nowhere near as popular as they had been in the 50s, when, along with westerns, they had been the most prolific genre of film in America.

The production was troubled, with constant overages driving up the budget. Finally, tired of what they were hearing, United Artists took over the editing and, by all accounts, including Scorsese's, butchered the film. The cut that premiered to audiences and critics was not what Scorsese intended, and he ensured everyone knew it. In 2004, he was offered the chance to present his version of the film for the Blu-Ray release, and he agreed.

With hindsight, many believe that had the Scorsese cut of the film been released in 1977, it would have been a hit. Not a monster hit like *Jaws* (1975) or *Star Wars* (1977), but a solid money maker.

Set and opening on V-J Day, marking the end of WWII, Francine (Minnelli) is partying with some friends in the city while Jimmy (De Niro) vies for her attention. He will not leave her alone. They end up sharing a cab, auditioning together, falling in love, and marrying. Her career takes off, and his does not—a tale as old as time.

Liza Minnelli is very good as Francine but doesn't match her pinnacle performance in *Cabaret* (1972). She never again rose to those heights. Although, had the film been screened according to Scorsese's vision in 1977, she might have found herself with another Oscar nomination.

De Niro gives the most annoying performance of his career. We hate Jimmy from his first appearance. He is arrogant, obnoxious, rude, and relentless, even when it hurts and wounds Francine, the woman he claims to love. The two could not be more different as people, yet somehow, Francine loves this loser. In fairness, De Niro captures every negative aspect of Jimmy, which is not an easy task for an actor. He is so intensely dislikable.

The sets and production design are surreal, giving the film a haunted look, as though it were all a dream or a memory. It was a bold choice and one that might have sabotaged the film. After bombing at the box office, it was ignored at the Oscars, receiving nothing, not even for the title tune, which has become one of the most famous songs ever written.

Though the executives didn't have much choice but to step in when Scorsese was imploding, it's such a shame that they also decided to cut his work. Scorsese proved to be a genius, and when he recut the film in the 2000s, his mastery became apparent. One of the most daring films of the decade, but terribly wronged by the studio.

"Tired of what they were hearing, United Artists took over the editing and, by all accounts, including Scorsese's, butchered the film."

160 SATURDAY NIGHT FEVER (1977)

DIRECTED BY John Badham
COUNTRY USA

Opposite Travolta becomes a superstar, Oscar nominated for Best Actor, and Lord of the Dance Floor.

Often described as "that disco movie," *Saturday Night Fever* deserves more. It is a powerful study of teen angst and aspirations, and the film turned John Travolta into a superstar. In the opening frame, the camera is ahead of Travolta as he walks down the street to the Bee Gees' hit "Stayin' Alive." He carries a can of paint, stops to put a deposit on a shirt, stops again for pizza, stacking one piece atop the other, and carries on, taking in the busy Brooklyn street as he walks back to the hardware store where he works.

Tony Manero (Travolta) lives with his parents in a crowded house in Brooklyn, chipping in to support the family. It is Saturday night, and he preens for the evening as if hypnotized: fixated on his hair, suit, and gold chains. He is on his way to 2001 Odyssey discotheque, where Tony is king of the dance floor. He might be a nobody on the street, but on the dance floor, he is a god, and he knows it. As the best dancer on the floor, he can have his pick of the girls. They swoon over him; one offers to wipe the sweat off his brow.

Annette, portrayed by Donna Pescow, sees him as the love of her life and wants him as more than a dance partner. He barely notices her.

All Tony thinks about is getting back on the dance floor, but he cannot afford more than one night out a week. A line from "Stayin' Alive" is "I'm going nowhere ..." and Tony feels that. He enters a dance competition with Annette but later catches the eye of a talented young dancer and chooses her instead. He and Stephanie (Karen Lynn Gorney) are terrific together on the dance floor, but Tony is not mature enough to be just friends and pushes for more intimacy. Stephanie likes being around him because it makes her feel better about herself. Like Tony, she is a Brooklyn girl. She has recently realized Tony's dream of crossing over the bridge to Manhattan but often feels like an outcast.

In the end, a tragedy intervenes, and Tony turns to Stephanie for support. For the first time, she sees him as more than a play toy, and he sees her as a friend.

Travolta was a revelation as Tony Manero. Famous dancer Gene Kelly praised his dance moves but also was impressed by his acting, as were the critics. Travolta received an Academy Award nomination for Best Actor, a fact that often gets overlooked. Only twenty-two years old and an exceptional actor, he seemed to have a promising career ahead of him. Still, after *Blow Out* (1981), arguably his finest performance, he disappeared into terrible films and B movies. His comeback came seventeen years after *Saturday Night Fever* with *Pulp Fiction* (1994).

Incredibly, the songs from the film received nary a glance from the Academy. "Stayin' Alive," "If I Can't Have You," and "How Deep Is Your Love" were all massive hits and Grammy Award winners, but the Academy did not embrace the songs. That year's winner was the insufferable "You Light Up My Life."

“Travolta received an Academy Award nomination for Best Actor, a fact that often gets overlooked.”

"Hill beautifully recreates life on the ice for his audience with all the speed and furious action."

SLAP SHOT (1977)

DIRECTED BY George Roy Hill
COUNTRY USA

Ironically, an American film studio created the cult classic about a game generally accepted as inherently Canadian. But, to their absolute credit, the movie perfectly captures the game's spirit. As a Canadian, I played ice hockey starting at the age of five and continued playing goalie for many years. I loved every second of my time in the net.

Writer Nancy Dowd followed a minor league ice hockey team on the road to glean information for her screenplay. She discovered the salty language in the dressing room and on the ice, the dangers of playing on razor-sharp blades, skating at speeds exceeding thirty kilometres an hour with hard wooden sticks, trying to smash a piece of vulcanized rubber past a goalie into a net.

George Roy Hill, Academy Award winner for *The Sting* (1973) and nominee for *Butch Cassidy and the Sundance Kid* (1969), directed the film, relying on star Paul Newman to make it realistic. He cast many real-life minor hockey players and one actor with a solid background in hockey, Canadian Michael Ontkean, who had tried out for the New York Rangers before quitting the game for good to be an actor. Hill got his inspiration from the "Broad Street Bullies" (the Philadelphia Flyers), who battered their way to two consecutive Cups.

The Charlestown Chiefs are a minor league team down on their luck. Amid a losing streak, rumours abound that the team is for sale and player-coach Reggie Dunlop (Newman) tries to intervene. He argues that "this is all these guys have" and "all the town has," but the truth is, it is all Reggie has too. He convinces his team to play the game rough, fighting their way to wins, to goon it up so they can earn headlines and attention. He brings in the hysterically funny Hanson Brothers, three rugged boys with identical glasses who terrorize the other teams.

And, of course, it works.

Paul Newman was in the twilight of his career but doing some of the finest work of his long history in movies. His performance as Reggie is among his finest; he is hilarious in the role. Young Ontkean is excellent as the team's conscience who turns out to be a sexual deviant in the bedroom, which we finally see when he strips down to his jock strap on the ice. Surprisingly, the real-life minor league players are excellent in their roles, demonstrating a decent amount of raw acting talent.

Hill beautifully recreates life on the ice for his audience with all the speed and furious action. Three years after the film's release, the 1980 American Olympic ice hockey team would stun the world by winning the gold medal, defeating the mighty Soviets, resulting in an emerging interest in hockey in the US. *Slap Shot* became a popular rental on video and is still a strong seller on Blu-Ray.

A hilarious comedy and one of the great, however irreverent, sports films ever made.

Opposite Written by Nancy Dowd, this tough, raunchy film about minor league hockey offered Paul Newman one of his finest roles.

"Critics were unkind to the film, but time has helped *Sorcerer*, and it is now often considered a masterpiece of 70s cinema."

SORCERER (1977)

DIRECTED BY William Friedkin
COUNTRY USA

At the height of his arrogance, after winning the Academy Award for Best Director for *The French Connection* (1971) and being nominated for *The Exorcist* (1973), William Friedkin was in Paris with actress Jeanne Moreau, dining with the great French director Henri-Georges Clouzot. Looking the French filmmaker directly in the eye, Friedkin announced that his next film would be an English language remake of *The Wages of Fear* (1953), the finest film Clouzot made.

And away Friedkin went to make his film, retitled *Sorcerer* (1977). Despite the title, it was not about anything supernatural. The sorcerer of the title referred to the name of one of two trucks transporting nitroglycerin across the rugged jungle and mountain landscape of South America. Audiences were confused, expecting something like *The Exorcist* and getting something entirely different.

Critics were unkind to the film, but time has helped *Sorcerer*, and it is now often considered a masterpiece of 70s cinema. Along with misleading audiences with its title, the release was hamstrung by having to compete with *Star Wars*. Audiences chose to pay for multiple viewings of that epic instead of seeing something new.

Sorcerer is a grand, intense adventure, gritty and powerful. On the run from men who want them dead, a quartet of criminals is hiding out in South America when presented with a proposition. They will need to transport some cases of nitroglycerin across the country in return for a great deal of money, enough to start again and disappear from the eyes of the men who are after them.

The film opens with four vignettes set around the world, where we meet the men portrayed by Bruno Cremer, Francisco Rabal, Amidou, and Roy Scheider, who each find themselves on the run for various reasons. They each accept the offer and are soon retooling the trucks to transport the nitro across the rough and unforgiving land.

Friedkin builds unbearable tension by reminding us of this liquid's volatility and explosive properties, bouncing around in the back of these unsteady trucks. After losing two of the men, Scheider is left to cross a dangerous rope bridge, guided by his remaining partner and his own instincts. He makes it, delivering the goods, but as he returns to the small town to collect his money, the men searching for him appear.

Stunningly shot, using the lush jungles as a perfect background, danger lurks at every turn. The slightest bump or a sudden turn could reduce the truck to ashes. The musical score by Tangerine Dream fits the tension brilliantly.

Unknown actors made up most of the cast, which worked well, although it wasn't Friedkin's first choice. He had hoped to cast Steve McQueen, but as McQueen did with *Apocalypse Now* (1979), he turned the project down, not wanting to be away from home for a year.

The actors he ended up with, Scheider especially, do an impressive job of showing the sheer terror and angst of this mission. They witness the power of their cargo when they use it to eliminate a tree that blocks the road.

Though it bombed at the box office, home entertainment helped bring *Sorcerer* to audiences, first as a VHS rental, then on DVD and Blu-Ray. Though an unusual film with a definite foreign-film feel, it is powerful cinema and a true classic of the 70s.

Opposite Roy Scheider (centre) leads a group of criminals across South America, hired to haul deadly nitroglycerin. Though a failure upon release, *Sorcerer* has become recognized through the years as a masterpiece.

STAR WARS (1977)

DIRECTED BY George Lucas
COUNTRY USA

Opposite Entering film legend, the heroes.

You could feel the energy in the cinema as the trumpets sounded and the words appeared with that famous story roll. A ship appears at the top of the screen, shooting at something behind it. It comes closer until the Star Destroyer fills the entire screen and swallows up the other ship. It was extraordinary.

Star Wars created a seismic shift in movies. It had a deceptively simple narrative—essentially a western in space with elements of *The Seven Samurai* (1954) merged with Flash Gordon and Buck Rogers. The pace was fast, and never let up. It was an instant classic, quickly becoming the highest-grossing film of all time.

The story begins with Luke Skywalker (Mark Hamill) as a young farmer on a distant planet dreaming of joining the rebellion. Following the murder of his aunt and uncle, he joins Obi-Wan Kanobi (Alec Guinness), previously a Jedi Knight, who returns to the Force to answer a message from Princess Leia (Carrie Fisher). They sign on with a space pirate, Han Solo (Harrison Ford), and off they go, chasing the rebellion.

Darth Vader, a black-cloaked creature who is a master of the dark side of the Force, captures them, and he and Ben end up in a lightsaber duel. Ben knows he will be more valuable dead than alive, plus his diversion allows Luke and Princess Leia to escape. With the help of Solo, they return to blow up the Death Star and send Vader spinning off into space, still very much alive. Luke and Han are decorated for their efforts, fulfilling Luke's dream, although he is light years from home.

The array of creatures introduced throughout the film delighted audiences. Lucas filled the screen with his wild imagination, from the heroic Wookie, Chewbacca, the droids C-3PO and R2-D2, to the aliens in that crazy bar. Yet, at its heart, *Star Wars* is simply a story about good versus evil.

Lucas was always a visionary first, a director second, and a writer third. The actors made the movie work. He barely spoke to them. But sometimes, actors don't require a lot of direction. Harrison Ford was perfect as the gruff anti-hero. Hamill was equally great as the wide-eyed, naive young man who becomes a hero. Carrie Fisher made her name as the feisty princess, and of course, who else but Alec Guinness could have played wily old Ben? James Earl Jones provided the ominous voice of Darth Vader.

Audiences went crazy for the film; nominated for ten Academy Awards, it won seven. And while it was a Best Picture and Best Director nominee, by the year's end, most agreed that it had been surpassed by *Close Encounters of the Third Kind* (1977), his good friend Steven Spielberg's film.

Star Wars has since become one of the most popular and successful franchises. The first trilogy, from 1977 to 1983, included *The Empire Strikes Back* (1980), still the greatest of the films, and *Return of the Jedi* (1983). In 1999, Lucas went back to directing the films and gave us *The Phantom Menace* (1999), *Attack of the Clones* (2002), and *Revenge of the Sith* (2005), the best of the prequels. When Disney purchased the rights to Lucasfilm, they kick-started the *Star Wars* series with their own trilogy in 2015, which saw the death of Han Solo in the first film, *The Force Awakens*.

It would be challenging to find a person who doesn't know the phrase, "May the force be with you." That would be quite an accomplishment.

"Lucas was always a visionary first, a director second, and a writer third. The actors made the movie work."

"The film is considered a landmark in the evolving history of films about women, particularly because she does not find happiness in the arms of a man at the end."

AN UNMARRIED WOMAN (1978)

DIRECTED BY Paul Mazursky
COUNTRY USA

Jill Clayburgh's astonishing performance as Erica in Paul Mazursky's *An Unmarried Woman* became the defining work of her career. The film is considered a landmark in the evolving history of films about women, particularly because she does not find happiness in the arms of a man at the end. Never again did Clayburgh reach such a remarkable height, nor box office success. She won the New York Film Critics Award for Best Actress and was nominated for an Academy Award, losing to Jane Fonda in *Coming Home* (1978).

Erica is married to an affluent New Yorker, portrayed by Michael Murphy. They have a good life together, a precocious teenage daughter with too many opinions, a great sex life, and a huge New York apartment. They are by all accounts happy. The film's opening moments have Erica, pretending to be a world-class ballerina, gliding through the apartment in a T-shirt and panties, sensual but also having fun. She rushes off to meet her husband for lunch, where he shatters their entire world. Crying on the street, he confesses he has been having an affair for nearly a year, is in love with the younger woman, and is leaving her. Erica is gutted. The breakup leaves her broken, cynical, and intensely bitter. She woefully struggles to find happiness through dating and caring for her daughter.

She throws her energy into her career as a very sharp art dealer. One night she beds a brooding artist portrayed by Cliff Gorman, more for the sex than anything else. She gladly walks away after. Later in the film, she meets a British artist, and they hit it off. Though they connect and work well together, she refuses to be defined by a man. She cannot allow that to happen to her again. Out of the blue, her ex-husband contacts her and wants to come home because his girlfriend has left him. Feeling nothing but pity for him, she says no. She has come too far ever to go back.

Male audiences in the 70s probably learned much from watching her journey and vulnerability. We root for her because she struggles, then rises through her pain and finds herself. That was the incredible power of the film and the brilliance of Clayburgh's performance.

Excellent reviews greeted the film, and three Academy Award nominations for Best Actress, Best Picture, and Best Screenplay, all richly deserved. Clayburgh's soaring performance remains among the finest of the decade, a remarkable piece of acting.

Opposite Sad and broken Erica (Jill Clayburgh) comforts her angry daughter portrayed by Lisa Lucas in Paul Mazursky's superb film.

170 AUTUMN SONATA (1978)

DIRECTED BY Ingmar Bergman
COUNTRY Sweden

Opposite Two acting titans, Liv Ullmann and Ingrid Bergman are extraordinary as estranged mother and daughter.

After several failed attempts, Ingmar Bergman was finally able to cast legendary three-time Oscar winner Ingrid Bergman in one of his films. Adding to his delight, he also chose Liv Ullmann as Bergman's daughter. A casting dream, the film at once became one of the must-see films of 1978.

Like all of Bergman's best films, it challenges audiences because nothing comes easy to his characters. With no magical Hollywood endings, European films seem to explore realism with more relish than Americans, though American filmmakers in the 70s evolved with influence from their European colleagues.

Eva (Ullmann) is the daughter of famous pianist Charlotte (Bergman), and she invites her mother to visit after a seven-year absence. Eva, by most accounts, is a formidable woman. She is married to the town's pastor, cares for her disabled sister, Helena (Lena Nyman), writes books, and is a respectable pianist. Despite her accomplishments, Eva will never measure up to her mother's expectations. Charlotte seems more shocked than impressed that Eva has selflessly taken Helena into her home to care for her.

Charlotte gifts Helena her watch and Eva her car. It's not a significant sacrifice; she carelessly announces that she will buy herself a new car when she returns home. They talk of the past and argue but accomplish little in healing their relationship. Eva is in pain and deep down resents that she is the caregiver to her sister, forced to be the substitute mother because Charlotte would not step into the role, abandoning her children for her career.

The film's conclusion offers a glimmer of hope. Or is it only in the characters' minds and not real? Ingmar Bergman challenges the viewer to decide for themselves.

The film was an immediate sensation in large markets in North America, especially Chicago, Los Angeles, New York, and Toronto, earning rave reviews from the nation's critics. Ingrid Bergman won Best Actress awards from the National Society of Film Critics, the National Board of Review, the New York Film Critics Circle, and an Oscar nomination for Best Actress. Though Liv Ullman matched her in every way, she was passed over while critics and the Academy fell over themselves to honour Bergman.

Widely considered one of Ingmar Bergman's greatest films, it arguably contains the two finest performances he ever guided. Powerful and forever haunting.

"Like all of Bergman's best films, it challenges audiences because nothing comes easy to his characters."

"Fonda specified that she wanted the story to be about the men returning home rather than a film about combat."

COMING HOME (1978)

DIRECTED BY Hal Ashby
COUNTRY USA

Commissioned by Jane Fonda, *Coming Home* was the first of a substantial batch of films about the war in Vietnam and its horrific impact on those who fought, those left behind, and, of course, the Vietnamese. The film marked Fonda's return to Hollywood after a long break. She decided to bring her protest against the war to the big screen, hiring Nancy Dowd (who wrote the profane script to *Slap Shot* (1977)) to write a screenplay about the war in Vietnam. Fonda specified that she wanted the story to be about the men returning home rather than a film about combat. Francis Ford Coppola was off in the jungles of the Philippines making *Apocalypse Now* (1979), and Fonda wisely decided not to create a movie that would try to compete with his.

She chose Hal Ashby to direct the film, Jon Voight to play Luke Martin, a former high school jock who returns home a paraplegic, and Bruce Dern as Bob Hyde, Fonda's hawkish husband who returns emotionally shattered by the war. Many of the supporting roles and extras were real Vietnam veterans whom Ashby met at the VA hospital where much of the film takes place.

Once Bob goes off to fight the war, Sally (Fonda) volunteers at the base hospital and soon realizes no one cares about the men once they return home. The hospital operates on a paltry budget, and the men suffer from hopelessness and despair. She remembers Luke from high school, and they begin a casual friendship, though it is clear Luke cannot take his eyes off her. After a trip to Hong Kong to visit Bob, she realizes he has changed and become disillusioned about the war. It certainly is not what he expected. In a hotel room, he walks in circles, telling her, "My men were chopping off heads because that's what they were into." She returns in time to bail Luke out of jail for a protest he staged over the death of a friend and goes home with him. They make love, and for the first time in her life, Sally experiences an orgasm. She and Luke fall in love.

Bob comes home and all hell breaks loose when the army informs him of what has happened between his wife and Luke. Armed, he verbally assaults Sally until Luke shows up, and he talks him down, saying, "You don't want to hurt anyone here; we've all got enough ghosts to carry around."

The final fifteen minutes of the film are a masterclass in editing. As Luke speaks truthfully to a group of high school kids about the war, breaking down at the remembrance of the experience, Bob is standing on his beach after being awarded a medal for bravery. We hear Tim Buckley's "Once I Was," a mournful song about loss, as Bob begins to undress, runs naked into the ocean, and disappears.

The performances in *Coming Home* are astonishing, powerful pieces of acting filled with truth. Jon Voight is remarkable as Luke, broken but trying to fit back into life despite the horrors he carries around. Fonda is superb as the initially naive young woman who learns so much in a short time and embraces the change, especially her new role as a liberated woman speaking out against the war. Dern is a powder keg who finally explodes in rage at the betrayals he perceives. He has lost his place in the world and cannot accept it. All three earned nominations for Academy Awards, and Fonda and Voight won Best Actress and Best Actor. The film received eight nominations, Best Picture and Best Director among them. *The Deer Hunter* beat them out for both, but *Coming Home* is a vastly superior film.

Opposite Jane Fonda, actress, producer, and driving force behind *Coming Home*.

174 GREASE (1978)

DIRECTED BY Randall Kleiser
COUNTRY USA

Opposite In the summer of 1978, *Grease* was indeed the word. John Travolta and pop artist Olivia Newton John delighted audiences, many returning two or three times to delight in the film.

In the summer of 1978, *Grease* was the word, an enormously popular musical with a fantasy take on high school in the 50s. Repeat viewings were common, and *Grease* became a huge success, second in box office ticket sales only to *Superman*.

Key to its success was John Travolta as Danny, fresh from an Oscar nomination for *Saturday Night Fever* (1977), pop princess Olivia Newton-John as good girl Sandy, Stockard Channing as bad girl Rizzo, Jeff Conaway (sadly gone) as Danny's best friend Kenickie, and a host of minor 50s stars in cameo appearances.

Grease was frothy, fast-paced, and fun, but nothing more. It is silly but ends with a disturbing lesson for young women. Change yourself to satisfy your man.

The film begins on the first school day after summer vacation and covers a group of students' final year. Danny is the leader of his gang, while Sandy is an exchange student who coincidentally ends up at his school after a summer romance with him. When they run into each other, Sandy discovers that Danny is a different person at school. He acts cool and disinterested in front of his friends. Stunned by his actions, Sandy wants little to do with him.

In the middle of the mess, stirring the pot, is devious Rizzo, who taunts and teases Sandy.

By the film's end, Sandy knows she wants Danny and is willing to do whatever it takes to get him. She decides she needs to transform her style by puffing up her perfectly coiffed hair and exchanging her preppy clothes for lots of skin-tight leather. She struts to show him she is now "his type." Of course, they get together and fly away in the hot rod Danny has worked so hard to create.

Yes, *Grease* is a ridiculous film, but it made a fortune at the box office, furthering Travolta's box office clout. The critics didn't take the movie seriously, but the executives at Paramount did as they watched their profits grow. The soundtrack was an even bigger hit, and the new songs in the movie were welcome additions to the already strong score. They received a nomination for Best Song for "Hopelessly Devoted to You," which was tailor-made for Olivia Newton-John's voice.

Travolta again commanded the screen as Danny. His confident swagger combined with a charming vulnerability proved a hit with audiences who enjoyed every one of his scenes. He also did his own singing, adding to his dancing and acting talent.

The role of Sandy was perfect for Olivia Newton-John with her fresh-faced innocence, and though there was nothing earth-shaking about her performance, she did a good job. Guys who were dragged to the movie on a date sat up during the dance scene with Sandy in her new look. Standing out in the cast was Stockard Channing, who was much older than high school age but pulled it off.

Grease was a graphic novel fantasy, reworked for the film. That explains the bizarre ending when the hot rod takes off into the heavens allowing them to be forever immortal, forever young.

"The critics didn't take the movie seriously, but the executives at Paramount did as they watched their profits grow."

HALLOWEEN (1978)

DIRECTED BY John Carpenter
COUNTRY USA

Opposite Michael Myers, the first of the serial killers in the slasher genre that emerged at the end of the 70s.

Horror cinema first emerged from Germany with its expressionistic film *Nosferatu* (1919), followed by the silent films of Lon Chaney, the Man of a Thousand Faces, and *Phantom of the Opera* (1925).

Universal Pictures jumped into horror with both feet in the 1930s, and their first productions became instant classics. *Dracula* (1931) and *Frankenstein* (1931) took America by storm and made stars of actors Bela Lugosi and Boris Karloff. Other films followed, such as *The Mummy* (1932) and *The Invisible Man* (1933), and then the plethora of sequels started. At first, they were brilliant. *The Bride of Frankenstein* (1935) far surpassed the original. But by the 1940s, the studio had taken to the unlikely grouping of the creatures together, finally pairing them with comedy team Abbott and Costello for a series of goofy films.

Then came *Psycho* (1960), in which the monster was the boy next door, a forerunner of the modern slasher films of which *Halloween* was the first.

By now, the story of escaped killer Michael Myers, he of the silly face mask rumoured to be a cast of William Shatner, needs no introduction. The lumbering maniac, armed with a knife but able to kill in just about any manner, became one of modern cinema's true monsters, with one sequel after another spanning over forty years.

The film made Jamie Lee Curtis a star, the first "Scream Queen" of the modern era, who went on to a fine career in film. The movie also introduced us to the talents of director John Carpenter, who made *Halloween* for a mere $300,000 and saw box office receipts of more than $80 million. He then directed the made-for-TV biography *Elvis* (1979) with a stunning Kurt Russell as Presley, *Escape from New York* (1981), and the cult classic remake of *The Thing* (1982).

Halloween gave birth to a cycle of films and their sequels, such as *Nightmare on Elm Street*, *Friday the 13th*, and then in the 1990s, the frightening *Scream* series.

The premise is simplistic; the film's power comes with its production, which elevated it to something truly terrifying. Michael Myers became one of the most frightening monsters in film history, later joined by such creatures as Freddy Krueger and Hannibal Lecter in modern films.

"The film made Jamie Lee Curtis a star, the first 'Scream Queen' of the modern era."

HEAVEN CAN WAIT (1978)

DIRECTED BY Warren Beatty and Buck Henry
COUNTRY USA

Opposite Soulmates? Warren Beatty romances real life love Julie Christie in this comic romance fantasy.

Make no mistake—Warren Beatty might have asked Buck Henry to help him direct, but Beatty was in charge. He had wanted to direct a film for many years. He proposed his biography of radical writer John Reed to Paramount (*Reds*, 1981), with him directing, acting, producing, and co-writing. He felt he should gain some experience directing one film in preparation. He chose to remake the fantasy film *Here Comes Mr. Jordan* (1942) and rewrote the screenplay with himself in the lead.

As Joe Pendleton, Beatty portrays a football star in the NFL for the Los Angeles Rams, in peak physical condition and about to bump the starting quarterback from his job as number one. Coming back from an injury with the help of the team's trainer Max Corkle, Pendleton is in the best shape of his career.

He gets hit by a car, and an over-zealous angel decides to pull him from his body to avoid unnecessary pain. When he gets to heaven, Joe insists a mistake has been made. They discover he is correct, but since his body has been cremated back on earth, they have a problem.

They place him in the body of a recently deceased millionaire, Joe Farnsworth, shocking his killers—his devious wife and his executive assistant. Knowing he cannot play football with Farnsworth's body, he begins to whip it into shape and brings his friend Max Corkle over to visit. Joe tries to convince Max that he is himself, divulging secrets to Corkle that only the two know, the final being what Max said at Joe's funeral to his dead friend: "I hope there's a football team in heaven, and I hope God makes you first string." With that, Max believes him, and they begin to train together. Farnsworth then buys the Los Angeles Rams. Though the players are dubious, Joe begins practising with them and takes a sound beating but doesn't give up. He makes a deal with them: they will give him a chance if he makes one play. Of course, he makes the play.

Along the way, Joe/Farnsworth falls in love with a young activist, Betty (portrayed by Julie Christie), while his wife and assistant continue their plot to kill him again. On the day of the Super Bowl, Joe learns he must give up Farnsworth's body. It was only a temporary arrangement. But the good news is, his new body is that of the Rams' quarterback, Tom Jarrett. The only catch is that he will become Tom and forget about Joe. Max arrives at the stadium in time for Joe to tell him it is indeed him inside Jarrett, but his memory quickly fades, and Max loses him again.

On his way out of the stadium, Joe/Jarrett encounters Betty, and the two hit it off. She remembers that Joe had warned her she would meet a quarterback one day and should go for a coffee with him. She smiles and agrees to have a coffee with Jarrett.

A wonderful farce with a happy ending, this fantasy was a huge box office hit with audiences who loved the ghostly love story. From the moment the poster appeared, featuring Beatty in grey sweats and wings looking down at a stopwatch, audiences eagerly anticipated the film. They got a charming, warm story about love, the afterlife, and second chances. Audiences wept with joy at the hopefulness.

Beatty gave a superb performance as Joe but was generous as a director with his actors, allowing them to do excellent work too. The cast was well chosen, with Dyan Cannon as the hysterical, treacherous wife and Jack Warden as Corkle, Joe's loyal friend. Charles Grodin was perfectly smug as the assistant having an affair with his boss's wife, and James Mason was excellent as the heavenly Mr. Jordan. Beatty and Henry directed a comedic ensemble that far surpassed the original film.

Beatty received four of the nine Academy nominations for Best Picture (as producer), Best Director (with Henry), Best Actor, and Best Screenplay (again with Henry). He was the first artist to earn four nominations for a single film since Orson Welles in *Citizen Kane* (1941). Beatty did it again with *Reds* (1981), winning Best Director for that superb epic.

The film won a single Academy Award for its

splendid Art Direction, which included a unique image of heaven, or rather the weigh station before heaven, a mass of swirling clouds, and a strange-looking aeroplane taking the deceased to their next destination. Simplistic but beautiful and ethereal.

This was one of the very best comedies of the decade.

"John Belushi was a comedic force of nature as Bluto, a character with few lines but a major attraction. One look at him and you knew this guy would do anything to be funny."

NATIONAL LAMPOON'S ANIMAL HOUSE (1978)

DIRECTED BY John Landis
COUNTRY USA

It's just a silly little film. We might make a couple of bucks. Let them do whatever they want."—Studio Executive

That silly little film cost just $3 million.The cast and crew received measly pay with no perks such as personal trailers for the stars. Filming wrapped up in under thirty days. Despite its humble beginnings, it would launch the genre of teenage sex comedies and gross-out films. Movies like *Porky's* (1981) would follow, though none would ever find the massive success of this film. It would go on to make $141 million in its first run.

The narrative of the film follows a group of young male college students, members of the Delta fraternity, the worst on campus, known for its sexual exploits, excessive alcohol consumption, and massive parties. They challenge every rule of the college and generally wreak havoc. They are the targets of the dean, who wants them suspended for life. Other fraternities also want them gone, despite being guilty of their own misdemeanours.

Scenes from this movie are still familiar today, from goofy pranks like the famous imitation of a zit, to the toga party, to their exploits at the homecoming parade. The movie launched careers for a number of the actors.

John Belushi was a comedic force of nature as Bluto, a character with few lines but a major attraction. One look at him and you knew this guy would do anything to be funny. Bluto was the master of parties for the fraternity and possessed a GPA of 0.0. When he is finally expelled, he wails, "Nine years of college down the drain!" Tim Matheson did well for himself, never a star but easily recognizable in many films and eventually the popular TV drama *The West Wing* as the philandering Vice President. Karen Allen is terrific as one of the girlfriends of the guys, cheating with her professor, played with a crazy leer by Donald Sutherland. This strange ensemble also included James Widdoes, Kevin Bacon, Stephen Furst, and Bruce McGill.

Animal House is by no means cinematic art. Still, it cannot be ignored for its overall impact on audiences, redefining a genre, and showcasing the talented but doomed Belushi, who would be dead in three years.

Director John Landis would land in trouble after three people died on the set of his film *Twilight Zone* (1983). Appearing in court smug and self-satisfied, he was subsequently banished from Hollywood. The zaniness of his movie lives on.

Opposite The animals of Delta House included rising star John Belushi. He would die of an overdose four years later.

INTERMISSION: THE BLOCKBUSTER EMERGES

The summer of 1975 marked the first Hollywood blockbuster, turning the industry upside down.

Steven Spielberg's *Jaws* was an immediate smash hit, earning excellent reviews, but became famous overnight for its staggering impact on audiences. Queues formed around the block, hence the term blockbuster, and it quickly surpassed *The Godfather* (1972) as the highest-grossing movie of all time. From that point on, studios were on the hunt for the next money-making blockbuster.

Blockbusters also changed the way the typical movie calendar worked. January through April became the dog days when the studios released films with a questionable appeal. They would get dumped into cinemas, and only rarely would one emerge as a hit. The blockbuster months were from May to August, when the kids were out of school, and date nights weren't restricted to weekends. Repeat viewings were more likely to happen with these popcorn movies—exciting and entertaining but not too taxing on the brain.

Prestige films came out in autumn, in what has become known as awards or festival season. Hollywood began to recognize the value of releasing their films at one of the major film festivals in New York, Toronto, Telluride, and Venice, where audiences included media and critics, building that all-important advance press.

The studios claimed summer dates often two to three years in advance. *Jaws* was quickly followed by *The Omen* (1976), *Star Wars* (1977), which surpassed *Jaws* at the box office, *Grease* (1978), *The Empire Strikes Back* (1980), *Raiders of the Lost Ark* (1981), and *E.T. the Extra-Terrestrial* (1982), which topped *Star Wars*.

The summer months were often dominated by two or three massive hits that jockeyed for box office glory. A few choice films even made it to the Oscars with nominations in several categories.

Though Spielberg and Lucas are considered the masters of the blockbuster, they weren't the only names behind these massive productions. *Rocky* (1976), *King Kong* (1976), *Slap Shot* (1977), *Superman* (1978), *Grease* (1978), *Kramer vs. Kramer* (1979), and *Apocalypse Now* (1979) were also hugely successful.

But no one would argue that both men excelled at making popcorn films that delighted audiences. Spielberg seemed to have his finger on the pulse of average movie-goers, knowing instinctively what they wanted to see.

Many critics of the time harped that the two whiz kids were creating mindless tropes, removing the need for thoughtful reflection or imagination. But as the studios poured big money into countless blockbusters that flopped, it became apparent that there was an art to this form. It required a good story and a solid script. That has always been the

Above The surprise hit of the summer of 1976 was *The Omen* featuring diminutive Harvey Stephens as Damien, the child of Satan. Unnerving and chilling, it was a huge hit establishing Richard Donner as a major director.

case. While the *Star Wars* trilogy was entertaining, it was hardly fluff, paying homage to the American western and the Japanese film *The Seven Samurai* (1951). Major films like *Jaws*, *Star Wars*, and *Close Encounters of the Third Kind* (1977) were great movies even before the creators added special effects and big sound to the formula.

When Spielberg sought more serious fare, he was not recognized as he had hoped, at least not initially. However, by the time he made *Schindler's List* (1993), a masterwork of cinema, he had grown substantially as a filmmaker. Earlier that same year, his *Jurassic Park* became the highest money maker of all time and forever altered the course of visual effects using computer-generated imagery.

Spielberg was always a great filmmaker and did not need to make only serious-minded films to prove that. His blockbuster hits showcased his growth as a director and an artist. The blockbuster did not put an end to the "auteur period" of the 70s, as some argue. What ended the second Golden Age of Hollywood was the obscene spending followed by significant failures of many movies in the decade. And, of course, *Heaven's Gate* (1980) was the most blatant example of self-indulgence and lack of respect towards a studio in Hollywood history.

"The blockbuster did not put an end to the 'auteur period' of the 70s, as some argue. What ended the second Golden Age of Hollywood was the obscene spending followed by significant failures of many movies in the decade."

"*Straight Time* was ignored by audiences when it was released in the summer of 1978 but not by critics."

STRAIGHT TIME (1978)

DIRECTED BY Ulu Grosbard
COUNTRY USA

The 70s was a time when great films seemed to be released weekly into cinemas across the world. Perhaps this explains why many fell through the cracks, missed by audiences despite outstanding reviews. They were often discovered in subsequent years on home video, which would explode in the early 80s and change the face of movies forever.

Straight Time belongs in that category.

Max Dembo (Dustin Hoffman) is a thief recently released after a stretch in prison. He is the kind of guy who sizes up everyone he meets, looking for weaknesses and vulnerabilities that he can leverage. He lies when he does not have to, perhaps to stay in practice, and despises all forms of authority. His parole officer, a condescending, smarmy man, rubs him the wrong way immediately and later is responsible for sending Max back to jail for a weekend without cause. Max gets his delicious revenge later, telling us everything we need to know: he is a career criminal who has no interest in being anything else.

Straight Time was ignored by audiences when it was released in the summer of 1978 but not by critics, who praised Hoffman's superb performance and the gritty realism of the film. Very few films have accurately covered the life of a career criminal, someone who cannot go straight despite the potential consequences. Max knows what it means to be branded a felon, to spend time in jail, but even that doesn't deter him. He cannot help himself; it is the only life he has ever known.

Dustin Hoffman is always at his best when he is portraying a character with a mean streak. In his greatest performance, as Michael Dorsey in *Tootsie* (1982), he has a nasty streak that he loses when he becomes Dorothy Michaels, a woman. That talent for playing humanity's dark side never served him stronger than in this film.

Among the first people Max encounters when out of jail is a member of his old gang, who has moved on from crime, married, bought a nice home, works at a legitimate job. Yet Max goads him into helping him with a robbery. The heist goes terribly wrong; the police kill his friend, and Max kills the driver, portrayed by Gary Busey, who botched the getaway.

Max masters the art of reading people, pushing their buttons, and convincing them to follow him, but he can't fix himself. Hoffman captures this irony beautifully. Among his greatest performances and worthy of an Oscar but sadly, he received no recognition.

The supporting performances were equally gritty and realistic, especially Harry Dean Stanton as his good friend, and Busey as the dim driver who blows the heist. Hoffman initially wanted to direct the film but found he could not do double-duty with acting. He asked stage director Ulu Grosbard, a master with actors, to step in as a favour.

A powerful little film that so few people know or have seen, *Straight Time* is a hidden gem that deserves to be found.

Opposite Brilliant but ignored by audiences, Dustin Hoffman's performance as a petty criminal is among the finest of his career.

SUPERMAN (1978)

DIRECTED BY Richard Donner
COUNTRY USA

Opposite Seeing him soaring high above the city, we believed a man could fly in *Superman*.

For months, the trailers hurtled us through the clouds with a voiceover declaring: "You'll believe a man can fly!" Finally, we land on the famous S-crest. Superman was coming. The most famous comic-book superhero was coming to the big screen in a new, big-budget film that promised to be definitive. The cast included Marlon Brando as Jor-El, Superman's biological father on the home planet, Krypton; Gene Hackman was Lex Luthor, the criminal mastermind; Canadian actress Margot Kidder was Lois Lane; and in the role of Clark Kent/Superman was Christopher Reeve, a handsome actor best known for his stage work. At 1.93 m and packing on 15 kg of muscle for the role, Reeve cut an imposing figure, but could he portray a superhero?

It would all depend on two crucial moments: when we see Reeve for the first time as Superman, and that first moment he flies. Director Richard Donner brilliantly worked both moments into the same scene in the film, and I remember watching breathlessly as it unfolded.

Lois (Kidder) has gone to the roof of the *Daily Planet* to catch a helicopter to the airport to interview the US President. The cables catch the legs of the chopper, leaving it hanging perilously over the edge of the building. Exiting the building stories below is Clark Kent. He sees Lois's hat on the ground, looks up, and springs into action. Finding no phone booth nearby (a priceless scene), he changes costumes in a revolving door, and there he is—Superman. He streaks toward Lois just as she falls, unable to hang on any longer, but he catches her. "It's OK, miss," he says politely, "I've got you." Lois looks down, then back at him, and replies, "You've got me? Who's got you?" Suddenly, the chopper breaks loose and plunges toward them. In full frame, Superman catches it with one hand, holding Lois in the other, and flies to the top of the building, setting them both down safely. He then disappears into the night as Lois faints.

In cinemas across everywhere, audiences exploded in applause.

Director Donner took the right approach, treating Superman as a god, and much of the dialogue implies a quasi-religious theme. Jor-El says, "I have sent them you, my only son." Later, Lois describes her experience as holding "hands with a god."

Reeve played the part with the perfect amount of humility, with just a hint of sarcasm when necessary. His real challenge was as Clark Kent. It is a marvel of slapstick performance. Who would ever suspect that this bumbling, hapless goof is Superman? He simply straightens up, removes his glasses, and becomes another man entirely.

Brando was suitably god-like as Jor-El, and Gene Hackman was terrific as Lex Luthor, the film's arch-villain. Only Ned Beatty, as Luthor's henchman, rang false with an over-the-top performance.

America was changing, coming out of Watergate and into a new patriotic phase. Feel-good movies like *Superman* and *Rocky* (1976) helped the movement. Though Superman has appeared on the screen many times since 1978, the late Christopher Reeve made the role entirely his own. He is Superman.

And many believed he could fly.

“Though Superman has appeared on the screen many times since 1978, the late Christopher Reeve made the role entirely his own. He is Superman.”

188

"It might be the most over-praised film of the decade and among the weakest Academy Award winners for Best Picture."

THE DEER HUNTER (1978)

DIRECTED BY Michael Cimino
COUNTRY USA

Michael Cimino's sprawling epic *The Deer Hunter* offers as much to be admired as despised. Though indisputably talented, Cimino was notorious in Hollywood as a pariah. Within two years of basking in the glow of the Academy Awards, he had become better known as the man responsible for the bankruptcy of one of the oldest existing studios, United Artists, with his $40 million self-indulgent western, *Heaven's Gate* (1980). Some argued that, had the Academy delayed their voting for a few weeks, *Coming Home* (1978) would have won Best Picture and Best Director, and *The Deer Hunter* might have gone empty handed.

Cimino also had a bad habit of lying. He reported that he was attached to a Green Beret medical unit while in Vietnam and had seen the devastating injuries left by the mind games of the Viet Cong. Not so. He had not been in the US military, and the closest he ever came to Vietnam was to shoot *The Deer Hunter* in Thailand. It would not be the first time he misled his public, nor the last.

He read a script entitled *The Man Who Came to Play* about a man who comes to Las Vegas to play Russian roulette for sport. He adapted that script and turned it into *The Deer Hunter*.

Critics complained about *The Deer Hunter*'s xenophobic treatment of the Viet Cong, portrayed as vicious, grinning murderers who force their prisoners of war to play Russian roulette while they gamble on the game. They are little more than savages in the film, cruel and vicious.

The first ninety minutes of the film are terrific. We get to know the men and their community. They are salt of the earth, hard-working blue-collar men, one of whom is getting married before they ship out to war. At the wedding of Steven (John Savage) and Angela (Rutanya Alda), we learn more about the men and their friendships. Later that night, Nick (Christopher Walken) asks Michael (Robert De Niro) to bring him home should he die in Vietnam. The men go off into the woods for one last deer hunt. These scenes beautifully portray real and believable relationships between a group of friends, fresh-faced and already facing their mortality.

However, once we cut to Vietnam, the film falls apart. We must suspend our disbelief to buy that all three friends end up in the same prisoner-of-war camp. Their captors force them to play Russian roulette. Michael and Steven manage to escape and return home (with Steven badly injured), but Nick stays in Saigon. He comes across an illegal game of Russian roulette in a back alley. When Michael discovers Nick is still in Saigon, he returns to bring Nick home, remembering his promise. He ends up playing Russian roulette with Nick, who is in a drug-induced haze. Nick suddenly recognizes Michael, puts the gun to his own head, and pulls the trigger. The friends gather once more to bury him and mournfully sing "God Bless America" in the bar.

Though the scenes in Vietnam seem far-fetched, they are still well made. The cinematography is excellent, and the editing is remarkable, especially the tension built during the torture scenes. Given a mediocre script, De Niro, Walken, Hurt, and Streep all offer fine performances.

Critics initially hailed *The Deer Hunter*, but once the falsehoods came out about Cimino, the support for the film diminished. In fact, it might be the most over-praised film of the decade and among the weakest Academy Award winners for Best Picture.

Opposite Though it has moments of striking power and startling intimacy among the characters, the xenophobia and false presentation of the Viet Cong took away from the power of the film. Director Michael Cimino never learned how to be honest. The most overrated film of the decade.

"Gould gives an outstanding performance, but the film belongs to Plummer."

THE SILENT PARTNER (1978)

DIRECTED BY Daryl Duke
COUNTRY Canada

Made on a shoestring budget at the height of the famous tax shelter years in Canada, *The Silent Partner* was never given its due as a first-rate thriller with fine performances from the cast and an Oscar-worthy supporting performance from Christopher Plummer as the villain.

The Silent Partner played in cinemas for a short time in Canada. In the US, Roger Ebert and Gene Siskel offered a glowing review on their new Chicago TV show, which attracted audiences there, and similar reviews helped ticket sales in Los Angeles and New York. Many American critics hailed the film the "sleeper of the year." It has earned a solid reputation as a fine film in the years since.

Miles Cullen (Elliott Gould) is a bored bank cashier putting in time, looking for something to happen, something exciting that will break up the drudgery of his everyday life. During the holiday season, a man dressed as Santa Claus hands Cullen a note making clear he is armed and wants money. He looks convincing. Earlier, Cullen had discovered that the bank was to be robbed, figured out who the robber was, and prepared to steal the money before the robbery happened. Filling a lunch box with cash, he sets it aside and gives the robber a much smaller amount before he flees. On TV that night, they report how much was stolen from the bank, and the robber, holding much less than reported, realizes he has been duped.

Arthur Reikle (Christopher Plummer) begins to stalk Cullen and threatens to kill him unless he hands over the money. Neither one can involve the police given what has occurred, and Reikle proves as relentless as he is dangerous. Breaking into Cullen's apartment, he kills his girlfriend Elaine, decapitating her on the glass of an aquarium, leaving Cullen to dispose of the body. Cullen finally relents and agrees to give Reikle the rest of the money. Reikle shows up, this time dressed as a woman, but again he is foiled after shooting Cullen, drawing in the bank security guard who protects Cullen by shooting and killing Reikle.

Christopher Plummer portrays one of the most dangerous characters I have ever seen in a film. In one unforgettable scene, he speaks through a mail slot, and all we see are his eyes, blazing bright blue, alive with madness. And that voice. That scene is the stuff of nightmares and probably haunted many movie-goers long after seeing the film. It is an astonishing performance because it is so wholly unexpected and also because he is so believable.

Gould gives an outstanding performance, but the film belongs to Plummer.

Daryl Duke builds tension and fright, finally exploding in violence, all captured in Curtis Hanson's superb screenplay. Like the best maple syrup, *The Silent Partner* was a special treat from Canada.

Opposite Bank cashier Elliott Gould tries to stay one step ahead of a vicious criminal trailing him in this Canadian thriller.

192

1941 (1979)

DIRECTED BY Steven Spielberg
COUNTRY USA

Opposite Gonzo fighter pilot Wild Bill (John Belushi) in Steven Spielberg's colossal but entertaining comedy flop *1941*.

How could it happen?

After *Jaws* (1975) and *Close Encounters of the Third Kind* (1977), the boy genius Steven Spielberg made a massive flop. Not just at the box office but with the critics, who crucified the film. At this point, all the prominent directors of the 70s, except for Francis Ford Coppola, had endured a horrific failure. Coppola's would come later with *One from the Heart* (1982).

Spielberg's failure, from which he learned so much about himself, was a complete shock to the industry. It left Spielberg humbled and forever cautious about spending the money of others and taught him never to produce a film without co-producers.

1941 was billed as a comedy, but many asked, "Is Steven funny?" There is humour within his films, but comedy, outright comedy, is a rare animal.

Loving the screenplay by film school graduates Bob Gale and Robert Zemeckis, the gung-ho director shopped around for actors, even passing the script to the legendary John Wayne. The ailing actor turned down the role, but not because of his health. He felt the film was unpatriotic and foolish, and urged the director not to make the film. Undeterred, Spielberg forged ahead, choosing to cast many comedic actors from *Saturday Night Live* and the Canadian version, *Second City*.

1941 opens with a familiar scene and with great promise. Virtually a shot-for-shot replica of *Jaws* (1979), with the same actress swimming, but instead of a shark attack, the periscope of a Japanese submarine comes up under her, taking her high into the air. The Japanese have come to attack Hollywood and find themselves gleefully looking at a naked young woman who is understandably terrified. From there, *1941* falls to pieces, becoming a study in chaos more than a movie and possibly the least funny comedy of the decade.

John Belushi shows up as a deranged fighter pilot, with Dan Aykroyd as a commander with a head injury. None of their work is funny, nor is the film. Most of the time is spent showcasing destruction scenes, fight sequences, and out-of-control soldiers behaving like proper fools.

The effects and production design are fine, but the film became tedious within minutes and torture by the last hour. The film eventually made money at the cost of up to $38 million, but the relatively poor attendance stunned Universal, leaving Spielberg licking his wounds.

Time has not improved the movie, especially knowing the kind of director Spielberg became. It still begs the question, "What was he thinking?"

"*1941* was billed as a comedy, but many asked, 'Is Steven funny?'"

194 ALIEN (1979)

DIRECTED BY Ridley Scott
COUNTRY USA/United Kingdom

Opposite Smart and resourceful Ripley (Sigourney Weaver) defends her ship from a deadly alien life form. A franchise was born and with Weaver, a star was born.

Hollywood was in the middle of a science fiction and horror movie craze. What Ridley Scott did with *Alien*, in combining the two genres, was nothing short of genius. *Alien*, at its core, is a big haunted-house movie with a monster, and Scott superbly guides us through a tension-filled thriller with enough big scares to cause the audience to jump in their seats.

"In space, no one can hear you scream," read the ominous tagline for the film. How right it was, and a great way to start building dread and genuine terror.

The first thing you notice about *Alien* is everything looks lived in. This is not a shining and gleaming spacecraft; the ship shows plenty of wear and tear. The *Nostromo* is a cargo freighter making trips into deep space to gather and deliver. Upon embarking, the crew goes into a hyper-sleep, like frozen animation, and automatically wakes up when close to their destination. On this adventure, they awake to a distress signal. They search out the source and discover an abandoned ship. Inside, they find something unidentifiable. It is an egg-shaped object that quickly attaches itself to a crew member's face and proves impossible to get off. Each time they try, the thing grips tighter around the man's neck.

The following day at breakfast, that same crew member awakens with the egg gone from his face. He seems unaffected, laughing and talking, but begins violently coughing and complaining of chest pains. The crew clears the table and places him on it when, without warning, a creature bursts through his chest, chittering at them. It escapes as the crew member dies, his chest torn open from the inside.

As the creature grows, they realize its blood is heavily acidic, burning through the floors of the great ship. Very quickly, it grows into a towering monster and begins killing crew members horrifically. The remaining crew realize their likely fate.

Eventually, it is just Ripley (Sigourney Weaver) who is left to fight the deadly monster, and she outsmarts it, blasting it into space.

Alien was an immediate hit with audiences, who evidently were happy to pay money to be terrified. Ridley Scott proved a master of building dread and tension throughout the film, wisely keeping the creature in the shadows so that we catch just glimpses of it. This subtle technique terrified audiences and critics, who championed the film. Scott bravely made a woman the hero at a time when great films about women were just beginning to happen. After asking all the leading actresses to be Ripley, he decided to go with an unknown. Sigourney Weaver did not disappoint, delivering a superb performance as a strong, resourceful woman.

The visual effects were superb, and the design, sound, and eerie music all served to enhance the film.

No one in space can hear you scream, but many heard the screams of fright in cinemas worldwide as *Alien* unfolded in front of them.

A franchise was born.

“***Alien*** **was an immediate hit with audiences, who evidently were happy to pay money to be terrified.”**

"A brilliant, dark film in which Fosse took enormous risks with his narrative."

ALL THAT JAZZ (1979)

DIRECTED BY Bob Fosse
COUNTRY USA

One of the most wildly imaginative films ever made, Bob Fosse's semi-autobiography *All That Jazz* is, like his other works, a glimpse into the entertainment industry, in this case, film and stage. Back in 1974, Fosse was a busy man. He was finishing the choreography and staging of *Chicago* while also editing *Lenny* (1974), his black-and-white film about Lenny Bruce, putting in eighteen-hour workdays. After that, he barely had time to seduce the myriad of dancers he met, raise his daughter, and make time for his girlfriend. A heart attack nearly killed him, but he survived.

However, Fosse used his recovery time and the associated nightmares and visions to create this film, which is an extraordinary journey across the landscape of his mind. He tells his life story in flashbacks to what appears to be an angel, dressed beautifully in white, portrayed by an ethereal Jessica Lange.

Joe Gideon (Roy Scheider) is the surrogate for Fosse, a visual replica, going through the same wake-up routine every morning (cigarette, eye drops, a few pills, a check in the mirror, saying, "It's showtime folks!"). He sometimes remembers to put the cigarette out before showering, but not always, but he never forgets the pills.

He is in the middle of choreographing and directing a new Broadway play, a piece of fluff he needs to make substantial, which he does by making it intensely sexual. Gideon juggles a regular girlfriend, a jealous ex-wife, and any number of girls he takes home from rehearsal. His daughter sees all and says nothing, but his ex-wife certainly does.

After rehearsal ends, he hops in a cab and heads to the editing suites to see the latest cuts of *The Stand Up*, hoping the team has come up with a better version than the last. After maintaining this brutal pace for a while, he suffers a massive heart attack and lands in the hospital. Looming over him, always in sight, is the angel who we know by now is the Angel of Death.

In one extended hallucination, Joe imagines a TV show saying farewell to him. The audience includes his family and friends, and the production numbers involve many of them. In a jarring conclusion, we see Joe silently moving towards the angel who stands smiling, and we cut, almost violently, to a shot of Joe in a body bag.

A brilliant, dark film in which Fosse took enormous risks with his narrative He chose to let Joe die, perhaps as a warning to anyone who loses perspective on work balance. The film was electrifying, superbly directed, and beautifully acted by Scheider and Jessica Lange. One weak component was Leland Palmer as Joe's ex-wife, who comes across as crass and vulgar. Watching the dance number Joe creates, can we honestly believe he would be with this woman? I could not believe it.

Lange was haunting in the film, and Ann Reinking was terrific as a version of herself (she dated Fosse for several years).

Neither Fosse for Best director nor Roy Scheider for Best Actor had much of a chance, given the competition that year. Nominated for nine Academy Awards, competing with Francis Ford Coppola for the third consecutive time, the film won four for Song Score Adaptation, Best Editing, Best Costumes, and Best Production Design. It was the third Fosse film to be a Best Picture nominee in the 70s.

The portrayal of backstage Broadway is sensational and very realistic. The cattle call that opens the film is astonishing, as we watch Joe weed the dancers out and come up with the best of them, and the one who gets a break so he can sleep with her. There's no business like show business.

Opposite In this stunning masterpiece, Roy Scheider portrays Joe Gideon, a thinly disguised Bob Fosse (who directed), trying to bat back death despite an obsession with drugs, cigarettes, booze, and sex. Scheider gave the performance of his career.

198 APOCALYPSE NOW (1979)

DIRECTED BY Francis Ford Coppola
COUNTRY USA

Opposite As Willard, actor Martin Sheen nearly died on set after suffering a massive heart attack, returning to give a brilliant performance in *Apocalypse Now*, the fourth Francis Ford Coppola masterpiece of the 70s.

From the second the swaying, impossibly lush jungle explodes into flames to the strains of Jim Morrison mournfully crooning "The End," Francis Ford Coppola transports his audience into the hell and madness of the Vietnam War. As he told the adoring press at the Cannes Film festival in 1979 where he first screened the film, "My film is not about Vietnam. My film *is* Vietnam. We were in the jungle with access to much money and equipment, and little by little, we went insane."

Coppola flew to Thailand to create the first major American film about the war in Vietnam, a full two years before *The Deer Hunter* and *Coming Home* (1978) were released, each film winning Oscars and stealing *Apocalypse Now*'s thunder. Coppola and his crew emerged from the jungle two years after they started, having experienced their own war. Just to name a few battles: a typhoon swept away their expensive sets; Coppola fired leading man Harvey Keitel in the first few weeks; his replacement, Martin Sheen, suffered a near-fatal heart attack; the government of the Philippines routinely called back the choppers on loan to the film. But most notable and disruptive of all were the bizarre behaviours of actors Dennis Hopper (usually stoned) and Marlon Brando (jaded and spoiled). It indeed was a miracle Coppola finished the job at all, never mind creating a masterpiece.

With its sweeping, epic size and yet intimate studies of the characters, Coppola puts the audience up close and personal in Vietnam. Using Conrad's *Heart of Darkness* as a template, the story follows Willard (Sheen) as he is sent upriver into Cambodia to assassinate a US Colonel gone insane. Colonel Walter Kurtz (Marlon Brando) is a highly decorated soldier who abandoned the military and now lives in a guarded temple. As Willard learns more about Kurtz and reflects on the lunacy of this war, he begins to question his orders. But he and his crew carry on.

They encounter Lieutenant Colonel Bill Kilgore (Robert Duvall), a fearless man who loves war, famously declaring, "I love the smell of napalm in the morning. It smells like—victory." On the beach, strutting as bullets whiz past and grenades explode around him, he does not flinch. Kilgore flies into a village at dawn, hellbent on destroying it so his men can surf.

One by one, the men on the boat die on the way to Kurtz, leaving only Willard, Lance (Sam Bottoms), and Chef (Frederic Forrest). Kurtz's men later murder Chef.

In the end, Willard spends time with Kurtz, begins to understand him, and realizes he wants to die. Willard slaughters him like the sacrificial cow the natives kill, hacking Kurtz to death with a machete, leaving him to gasp out, "the horror, the horror."

Apocalypse Now galvanized its audiences, leaving us stunned by the terrible beauty of the film and the madness of war. Far superior to any film released at that time about Vietnam, it was hailed a masterpiece.

The performances of Martin Sheen, Robert Duvall, Marlon Brando, and Frederic Forrest were sublime. Coppola even drew brilliance from Dennis Hopper.

Nominated for eight Academy Awards, including Best Picture, Best Director, and Best Supporting Actor (Duvall), the film won just two, for Best Cinematography and Best Sound. It is still galling to realize that *Kramer vs. Kramer* won instead. And Coppola, for his astounding directorial achievement, won nothing despite a Directors Guild Award nomination and his third Oscar nomination for Best Director.

The breathtaking cinematography of the gifted Vittorio Storaro remains among the most stunning ever put on film.

A dark, startling work of art.

"Far superior to any film released at that time about Vietnam, it was hailed a masterpiece."

200 BEING THERE (1979)

DIRECTED BY Hal Ashby
COUNTRY USA

Opposite Hal Ashby's final great film of the decade is a biting, superb political satire in which a simpleton rises among the ranks of the White House. Peter Sellers gave the performance of his career as Chance, along with Shirley MacLaine as Eve Rand.

Can a feeble-minded man, lacking intellect, social graces, and knowledge of policy or a world map, lead a country?

We already know it can happen, just as we know the inherent damage it can cause when the public misjudges or overestimates someone they see as a leader.

In *Being There*, our emerging world leader is named Chance (Peter Sellers), a simple, gentle gardener who speaks in metaphors that people interpret as sage insight applicable to world affairs. He is supported by a benefactor, living in his home, and caring for his garden. When his benefactor unexpectedly dies, Chance is left homeless. He takes one of the old man's suits, his best overcoat and hat, and ventures out for the first time. When a car hits him, his life takes a turn.

Inside the car sits a wealthy lady. She mistakenly thinks he has introduced himself as Chauncey Gardiner when he says, "Chance the gardener." When she offers to take him home to convalesce, he happily accepts. It turns out she is married to Ben Rand, a wealthy, much older man who is the US President's (Jack Warden) best friend. Seeing Chance's fine clothes, Rand believes him to be well educated, wise, and very insightful about matters of the world. He has no clue Chance is ignorant of everything except his garden and watching TV.

The President visits his friend one day, and Chance is in the room listening, though not comprehending. They turn to Chance and ask him about the American economy. He answers, "As long as the roots are not severed, all is well. And all will be well in the garden. In the garden, growth has its seasons. First, come spring and summer, but then we have fall and winter. And then we get spring and summer again." Of course, he is speaking literally about his garden, but they quickly interpret his words as a clever metaphor. They think he is a genius.

Ben dies, but not before asking Chance to take care of his wife, and before long, he becomes a much sought-after political commentator. At Ben's funeral, the pallbearers exchange whispered comments that Chance should run for president. In the breathtaking final scene, Chance appears to walk across a pond of water, stopping to dip his umbrella deep into the water around him. Could he be the purely good leader the world has been waiting on?

Hal Ashby brought this fantastic fable to the screen after reading the best-selling Jerzy Kosiński novel. Many consider this to be Peter Sellers at his best. He masters both the blank stare and a look of passion when discussing his beloved garden. Sellers was an Academy Award nominee for Best Actor, and his co-star Melvyn Douglas won Best Supporting Actor for his performance. Shirley MacLaine and Jack Warden do excellent work, but the film belongs to Sellers, who is otherworldly in his brilliance.

The film was nominated for its superb Screenplay Adaptation and is considered the last truly great film directed by the wonderful Hal Ashby. An absolute masterpiece.

"The film belongs to Sellers, who is otherworldly in his brilliance."

“An explosive, divisive musical about the reaction to Vietnam, the play had been a controversial sensation on stage.”

HAIR (1979)

DIRECTED BY Miloš Forman
COUNTRY USA

It must be intoxicating to win a Best Director Award for the first time. It typically comes with a new level of recognition: you get meetings with the major studios and previously rejected projects are reconsidered. Such was the case with Miloš Forman. Fresh from an Oscar for his masterpiece *One Flew Over the Cuckoo's Nest* (1975), he shocked the industry by making a film of the classic cult musical *Hair*, a Broadway smash hit during the height of the counterculture wars. An explosive, divisive musical about the reaction to Vietnam, the play had been a controversial sensation on stage.

Was there any work of art more representative of the 60s? And that was precisely why the studios thought Forman was making a mistake. Could a movie ten years removed from the time it was popular still find an audience? The studios saw *Hair* like lightning in a bottle; its time was fleeting, and by the mid-70s, it was all but over. Forman persisted, and United Artists paved the way. With a rewrite for the screen, *Hair* hit cinemas in early 1979.

Incredibly, Forman and choreographer Twyla Tharp managed to bring the live, frantic energy of the stage production to the screen in a decisive manner.

We open with an Oklahoma farm, where Claude (John Savage) is leaving for New York City to report for duty to fight in Vietnam. He gets as far as Central Park, where he encounters a group of hippies, and Claude quickly becomes immersed in the Age of Aquarius. The extraordinary dance numbers by Tharp feel free, loose, as though created on the spot rather than having been carefully rehearsed (which was the case). Adopted into the carefree band led by Berger (Treat Williams), Claude spends his first night in New York in Central Park getting stoned. The merry band crashes a socialite's coming out party the next day, Berger climbing on the table and singing "I Got Life" and getting them all arrested and sent to jail. Trusting Berger, Claude gives him money to get them released, and to their surprise, he does.

Claude leaves to join the army. Berger and his friends drive across the country to the army barracks and sneak him out for a final rendezvous. Tragically, while Claude is partying, the barracks begin emptying out as the men are called to war. Berger is trapped and cannot do anything but board the plane in Claude's place. He leaves for Vietnam as Claude arrives to see the plane soar into the heavens. Later, the friends gather at a grave in a massive cemetery where Berger rests, killed in Vietnam. The unrest in the nation continues as the youth protest this foolish war.

One of the most beautifully edited sequences comes as Berger is marching towards the huge plane to take him to Vietnam, as the song "Let the Sunshine In" slowly builds to a massive choral sound. Standing over Berger's grave, they celebrate his life. Let the sunshine in indeed.

Forman stages the songs exquisitely, perfectly merging them with the narrative. His choice of songs was perfect. Some from the play did not make the film, though they were shot and recorded for the soundtrack album.

The film teems with energy, the burning restlessness of the youth of the 60s. This new generation doesn't trust their government or anyone over thirty, speaks their mind through protest and detachment, and breaks free of the chains of convention.

Despite excellent reviews, *Hair* was a box office failure, yet was discovered on video and then Blu-Ray. Today, it deservedly stands among the greatest musicals ever made.

Opposite Twyla Tharp's explosive choreography in *Hair* perfectly captured the essence of the youth rebellion of the 60s in Miloš Forman's breathtaking musical

204 KRAMER VS. KRAMER (1979)

DIRECTED BY Robert Benton
COUNTRY USA

Opposite Less a film about divorce than a love story between a father and son, Dustin Hoffman won a richly deserved Oscar for Best Actor and his co-star and movie son Justin Henry was nominated.

Portraying divorce realistically on film had not been something Hollywood was willing to embrace. They feared that the subject would be too difficult to watch, and no one wanted to take that risk. *Kramer vs. Kramer* did not shy away from the pain or ugliness but softened the plot with a love story between a father and a son, something utterly unexpected by critics and audiences.

Ted Kramer (Dustin Hoffman) is a hotshot advertising executive who comes home one day to find his wife Joanna (Meryl Streep) packed up and preparing to leave him. She barely keeps it together while telling him this, so anxious is she to leave this apartment that has become a prison to her. He is stunned, having had no idea how unhappy his wife was.

The following day, his son, Billy (Justin Henry), wakes to find his mother gone and his father now the primary parent. Reeling from the shock of his mother leaving, Billy acts out as Ted flounders. He realizes he does not have a clue about being a parent and needs to be more present with his son.

He adjusts his priorities to focus on his son and, in doing so, loses his job. Billy comes to mean everything to Ted, and the child grows to love his father equally. Just as they begin to find their groove, Joanna reappears, wanting to gain custody of Billy. This is a much different Joanna than Ted lost: she is confident, together, and with a job paying more than his.

In court, Ted's lawyer tries to tear Joanna down, focusing on her abandonment of Billy. Joanna hears from his lawyer and her best friend how Ted has changed and how he has cared for Billy. She is angry when her lawyer takes a cheap shot at Ted for an injury Billy sustained in his care. With both parents making passionate pleas as to why the boy should be with them, the judge rules on the side of motherhood. Devastated, Ted prepares to deliver his son to her and, worse, tells Billy he will need to leave to be with his mother.

On the day he is to go, Joanna comes and asks to speak to Ted downstairs. She has come to realize Billy is at home with his father, and together, they have built a life; she cannot tear him from that. She loves Billy enough to do the right thing.

Hoffman and Streep are both beyond brilliant. Hoffman's evolution from a work-obsessed, self-absorbed lout to a caring and loving father is a work of performance art, perfectly enhanced by the work of Justin Henry as Billy. The two actors feed off each other, and they create magic together. Watch the last scene they have, making French toast, waiting for Joanna to pick Billy up. So different from the first scene. They are in unison, and the grief they are experiencing is overwhelming.

Benton allowed Hoffman and Streep to write their own monologues for the courtroom scenes, each doing so brilliantly, though the win would go to Streep. In this sequence, she conveys her character's evolution, recognizing that her state of mind when she left Billy was unsuitable for raising a little boy, showing us how far she has come. But she also acknowledges the changes in Ted and is quietly stunned to see how he loves his son.

Hoffman swept the major acting awards that year, winning the Academy Award, the Los Angeles and New York Film Critics Awards, the National Society of Film Critics Awards, and the Golden Globe. His co-star Meryl Streep came into her own in 1979 as the screen's great new actress, winning all the same awards in the Supporting Actress category and adding an award from the National Board of Review.

Kramer vs. Kramer was nominated for nine Academy Awards and won five, including Best Picture, Best Director (Robert Benton), and Best Screenplay. Benton's victory meant that Francis Ford Coppola lost for *Apocalypse Now*, and I have never believed Benton achieved more than Coppola.

That said, critics, the public, and the Academy embraced the film's stunning realistic approach to its subject. It was a massive hit at the box office and remains among the finest American films ever produced about divorce.

"The two actors feed off each other, and they create magic together."

"Its success is especially remarkable given that this was a time of widespread homophobia, and many were uncomfortable seeing two men together on screen, touching, hugging, and kissing."

LA CAGE AUX FOLLES (1979)

DIRECTED BY Édouard Molinaro
COUNTRY France

This little French comedy became an international money machine, to everyone's surprise. Who could have guessed it would become a huge Broadway musical that won six Tony Awards, along with two award-winning revivals and a hugely successful film remake entitled *The Birdcage* (1996), starring Robin Williams and Nathan Lane?

Its success is especially remarkable given that this was a time of widespread homophobia, and many were uncomfortable seeing two men together on screen, touching, hugging, and kissing. We have come a long way since *La Cage aux Folles* first tickled our funny bone.

The original film was released in 1979 and was an immediate hit with audiences and critics in North America who embraced the hilarious lead characters.

Albin or "Zaza" (Michel Serrault) is the star attraction of the drag show he and his partner Baldi (Ugo Tognazzi) operate in a French resort town. The cabaret club is enormously popular, and Zaza is the show's star, but he is also a massive diva, high-strung, emotional, and wildly over the top.

Baldi has to deal with Albin's temperamental tirades, often just before he goes on the stage, or when he suspects Baldi is cheating, or when a fellow performer doesn't follow his directions. He is worse than a diva; everyone agrees he is a nightmare. Enter Baldi's son announcing his engagement and a planned dinner with his future in-laws. They begin to plot how they can avoid any embarrassing scenes from Albin. As a further complication, Baldi invites his son's birth mother to the evening even though she has not seen the boy in twenty years. A recipe for disaster? Sure enough, all hell breaks loose in front of the ultra-conservative in-laws.

Serrault is hilarious as Albin or Zaza, depending on his mood. It is a superb comic performance, just enough over the line to be hilarious. As the long-suffering partner Baldi, Tognazzi is wonderful, trying to be calm, but at the end of his rope with his unpredictable partner. Everything about the couple screams gay before such things were truly permitted. The release was just before the AIDS epidemic and years before legalized gay marriage in North America. Audiences emerged from the cinema with sore bellies, awakened to the fact two men could have a marriage like Lucy and Desi.

After winning the Golden Globe as Best Foreign Language Film, the film was a strong box office hit in North America and earned three Academy Award nominations for Best Director, Best Screenplay Adaptation, and Best Costume Design. It came away empty-handed, but two sequels followed, both hits, and then it became an industry with the Broadway musical and the Mike Nichols film.

Opposite The French film that spawned a franchise, including two sequels, a Tony Award winning Broadway musical, and an American remake entitled *The Birdcage*. The first was a smash hit in North America.

INTERMISSION: WOMEN IN FILM IN THE 70s

With the sexual revolution and women's liberation came new opportunities for women on screen. Women were slowly being cast in roles where they could be as authentic, genuine, and compelling as male actors. It was the first time in history the two were equals.

"I am woman, hear me roar," sang Helen Reddy. Around the globe, women dazzled audiences, demonstrating an astounding range of talent in bold new films. Here are the best and brightest with their contributions.

JANE FONDA Her performance in *They Shoot Horses, Don't They?* (1969) won her the New York Film Critics Award as Best Actress, and an Oscar nomination. Two years later, her performance as a stalked hooker in *Klute* (1971) earned her both awards. With an astounding piece of acting that is gritty and real, Fonda led the way for so many women who would follow. She forever altered how women were perceived. She then walked away from film for five years, coming back with a vengeance in *Fun with Dick and Jane* (1977), *Julia* (1977), *California Suite* (1978), *Coming Home* (1978), and *The China Syndrome* (1979). No one had the impact that Fonda did, and no one was better in the 70s.

ELLEN BURSTYN From the revered Actors Studio to the screen, Burstyn was realistic and rock solid. *The Last Picture Show* (1971) first revealed her gifts and earned her Academy and Golden Globe nominations. It was followed by *The King of Marvin Gardens* (1972), *The Exorcist* (1973), and her Oscar-winning performance in *Alice Doesn't Live Here Anymore* (1974). *Same Time, Next Year* (1978) and *A Dream of Passion* (1978) would make her an acting legend. She is still at work fifty years later.

PAM GRIER The first great black actress to triumph at the box office, Grier was beloved as *Foxy Brown* (1972) and in a host of trashy B movies in which she was ALWAYS the best thing on the screen. Strong, proud, sexy, and black, she was a formidable force of nature. Grier made a comeback in the 90s for Quentin Tarantino in *Jackie Brown* (1997) for which she was robbed of an Oscar nomination she so deserved.

BARBRA STREISAND By the time she entered the 70s, she was already an Oscar winner for her film debut in *Funny Girl* (1968), tying for the award with the great Katharine Hepburn in *A Lion in Winter.* Streisand was superb in the early 70s in *The Owl and the Pussycat* (1970), *The Way We Were* (1973) and *For Pete's Sake* (1974). By the time she appeared in *A Star Is Born* (1976), though she continued to be fabulous, her ego often got the best of her. She moved to directing in the 80s and 90s and was a natural. And that voice!

JILL CLAYBURGH The only issue with Jill Clayburgh is that she made too few movies. Her ravishing Carole Lombard in *Gable and Lombard* (1976) and *Silver Streak* (1976) got her noticed, and she was astonishing in *An Unmarried Woman* (1978), one of the best performances of the decade. Clayburgh was bold and daring in the incest drama *La Luna* (1979) and finished the decade with an Oscar nomination for *Starting Over* (1979). Her work in subsequent decades never matched her work in the 70s.

GLENDA JACKSON This British actress won two Academy Awards for Best Actress in the 70s, just three years apart, before leaving acting to become a politician. She was remarkable in *Women in Love* (1969), *The Music Lovers* (1971), *Mary, Queen of Scots* (1971), and *Sunday Bloody Sunday* (1971) before successfully trying her hand at comedy with Walter Matthau in *House Calls* (1978). Only recently are we seeing her return to the screen.

FAYE DUNAWAY After astonishing audiences and earning her first Oscar nomination with *Bonnie and Clyde* (1967), Dunaway enjoyed her time in the 70s as the lady of the moment. *Little Big Man* (1970), *Oklahoma Crude* (1973), *Chinatown* (1974), and the superb *Network* (1976), which won her the Academy Award for Best Actress. Never again would she be as bright a star as she was from 1967 to 1976 when she became a grande dame.

MARSHA MASON The wife of playwright-screenwriter Neil Simon broke through with a performance as a tough, unsentimental hooker in *Cinderella Liberty* (1973), earning an Oscar nomination. She followed it with mostly Simon films, earning nominations for both *The Goodbye Girl* (1977) and *Chapter Two* (1979). A favourite among critics in the 70s, she had a terrific decade but then declined rapidly.

LIV ULLMANN Ullmann was both a gifted screen and stage actress, and the muse to Ingmar Bergman. North American audiences loved her work, and her movies were solid hits for foreign language fare. Her expressive face and beautiful, soulful eyes were a canvas for the actress. She was Sweden's version of Jane Fonda. *Cries and Whispers* (1972), *The Emigrants* (1972), the wretched *Lost Horizon* (1973), *The New Land* (1973), *Scenes from a Marriage* (1974), *Face to Face* (1976), *The Serpent's Egg* (1977), and *Autumn Sonata* (1978) all contributed to her achievement as one of the world's greatest actresses. Truly brilliant.

DIANE KEATON From the comedies of Woody Allen to dark and disturbing films, Keaton displayed an astonishing range. *Play It Again, Sam* (1972), *The Godfather* (1972), *The Godfather Part II* (1974), *Love and Death* (1975), and *Annie Hall* (1977), for which she won an Oscar. She interrupted her string of comedies with a significant pivot to *Looking for Mr. Goodbar* (1977), winning her a Golden Globe nomination, and then returning to Allen with *Manhattan* (1979). Keaton evolved into one of cinema's best actresses, demonstrating an incredible staying power throughout the 70s and beyond.

TALIA SHIRE First cast as Connie Corleone in *The Godfather* (1972) and *The Godfather Part II* (1974), Francis Coppola's baby sister was outstanding. When she starred with Sylvester Stallone in *Rocky* (1976) and *Rocky II* (1979), and the drama *Old Boyfriends* (1979), she became a household name.

SALLY FIELD For years in primarily comedic roles on television, she broke out with *Stay Hungry* (1976) and then with Burt Reynolds in *Smokey and the Bandit* (1977) and the sequel. She also appeared with Reynolds in several of his other vehicles and, in between, gave a compelling performance in *Sybil* (1976) as a woman with multiple personalities, stunning her critics. In 1979 she swept most of the awards for that year with her seething performance in *Norma Rae* as a blue-collar worker who leads a union campaign. Still brilliant and still working.

BETTE MIDLER Just one narrative film in the late 70s thrust Midler into the limelight and earned her an Oscar nomination. *The Rose* (1979), based very loosely on the life of Janis Joplin, made Midler an actress, and she seized the role with abandon, utterly brilliant. The Divine Miss M, as she was known on stage, had arrived.

JODIE FOSTER A gifted child actress with many credits to her name by the time she hit her teens, she was catapulted to stardom by Martin Scorsese's dark *Taxi Driver* (1976). The very mature Foster, just thirteen, portrays a twelve-year-old hooker. Nominated for an Oscar, she was on her way and by the 90s had become one of the screen's greatest actresses.

210 MANHATTAN (1979)

DIRECTED BY Woody Allen
COUNTRY USA

Opposite Woody Allen's lyrical love story and valentine to New York is his best film of the 70s. The breathtaking black and white cinematography showcases the city in all its glory and the performances of Diane Keaton, Mariel Hemingway, and Allen are as always superb.

Despite his prolific production of movies in the forty years since the release of *Manhattan*, it remains Woody Allen's finest work. It is also the most visually beautiful film—shot by Gordon Willis, "the Prince of Darkness," in glorious black and white. Willis had famously shot both of Coppola's *The Godfather* films, infamously using darkness for its strategic effect. The black and white snapshots perfectly capture this glorious city, bringing out the romanticism, the past connecting to the present with breathtaking perfection.

When *Manhattan* opened, critics raved that it could be the best American comedy ever made. Allen landed on the cover of *TIME* Magazine, celebrating his genius.

Once again, Allen draws from his own life for the narrative. He is Isaac, a forty-two-year-old TV writer who has made a fine living. He is currently dating a seventeen-year-old high school senior, Tracy (Mariel Hemingway), while his best friend, Yale (Michael Murphy), is having an affair with Mary (Diane Keaton). When Isaac meets Mary, he dislikes her snobbery and haughty attitude toward modern art. However, they meet by chance again at an event without their partners and wind up talking through the night, ending on a park bench watching the sunrise at the Queensboro Bridge. Yale ends his affair with Mary, Isaac ends things with Tracy, breaking the girl's heart, and he and Mary begin seeing each other. Within a few weeks, she moves into his apartment.

Later, Yale and Mary get back together. Stunned and angry, Isaac confronts Yale, who childishly ends the argument with, "I saw her first." Realizing how much Tracy loved him, he runs to her apartment to find her leaving for six months in London. Begging her not to go, she says, "It's only six months... you have to have a little faith in people." Tracy proves to be the most mature of the lot of them.

Once again, Allen creates a love story with a bittersweet ending, just like life. The enchanting music of George Gershwin beautifully accompanies the movie. Spectacular!

The entire cast is sublime. Best of all is Keaton as the aggressive, neurotic Mary, and Hemingway as her complete opposite, the nurturing and loving Tracy. Meryl Streep had a small role as Isaac's ex-wife, who writes a humiliating best-selling book about their marriage. With her baleful glare and intense dislike for her ex, Streep was a formidable character in the film. Pity there wasn't more of her.

Some said the relationship in this film between Isaac and his much younger girlfriend paralleled real life and his marriage to Soon Yi. Although many believe Mia Farrow's accusations that Allen is guilty of sexual abuse against his adopted daughter Dylan, he was not tried nor convicted. But Hollywood, evidenced by his inability to distribute his movies, seems to have turned on him.

Despite the glowing reviews *Manhattan* received, it received just two Academy Award nominations, Best Supporting Actress (Hemingway) and Best Original Screenplay (Allen and Marshall Brickman). Allen was a Directors Guild of America nominee for Best Director and won Best Director Awards from the National Society of Film Critics and the New York Film Critics Circle.

Since *Manhattan*, Allen has made many truly great films but has never managed to surpass this, his finest film. As Chaplin's *City Lights* (1931) was to him, this is Allen's masterpiece.

“When *Manhattan* opened, critics raved that it could be the best American comedy ever made.”

212 NORMA RAE (1979)

DIRECTED BY Martin Ritt
COUNTRY USA

Opposite Urged by Burt Reynolds to take the role, Sally Field evolved into her character to absolute perfection and won every acting award for an actress that year, including the Academy Award. One of cinema's greatest performances.

By 1979, it was commonplace to have women in leading roles. So many films celebrated the growing role of women in society.

Jane Fonda broke down the door with her memorable performance as a hooker in *Klute* (1971), proving women could carry a movie in the lead role. Alongside her were other forces of female power, such as Barbra Streisand, Diane Keaton, Isabelle Adjani, and Liv Ullmann. One year after Fonda won her second Academy Award for Best Actress, an unlikely newcomer to film did the same.

Few in the film business took Sally Field seriously as an actress before 1977. Who could blame them? *The Flying Nun*? *Gidget*? *The Girl with Something Extra*? She was cute and petite, with big brown eyes and a lovely smile. Still, these TV sitcoms did not exactly showcase Field's abilities or inspire casting directors. Sometimes there is a lot to be said for courage, and Field dared to work in silly sitcoms and deliver fine performances. The instructors at the Actors Studio in New York recognized her potential and recommended her as the woman with multiple personalities in the TV movie *Sybil*. Field was astounding, earning rave reviews and attracting the attention of movie casting directors, filmmakers, and executives. More importantly, she won an Emmy, earning the respect of her peers.

She began to get decent screenplays, and one of them, *Norma Rae*, interested her. Burt Reynolds, her boyfriend both on and off the screen, read it and reportedly looked up at her and said, "And the winner is..."

Field must have felt the earth move under her feet when the reviews for *Norma Rae* came out because they would alter her career trajectory. Not only did she win the Academy Award as predicted by Reynolds, but the Los Angeles Film Critics Award, the National Society of Film Critics Award, the New York Film Critics Award, and the Golden Globe (Drama) for Best Actress. Not since Jane Fonda in *Klute* had an actress so swept the year-end awards.

Norma Rae is a single mother of two children by two different fathers, living with her parents in a crowded home in Alabama. She works alongside the rest of her family in sweltering heat in the local cotton mill factory, where the conditions are terrible, hours are long, and the pay measly. But it's the only gig in town. She tries a job as a foreman of sorts but is forced to report on her family and friends and will not do it. Known as a girl with a reputation and a past, she is stunned when Sonny (Beau Bridges), a loyal, hard-working single dad, proposes to her. She accepts, and soon after, Reuben (Ron Leibman) arrives in town to organize a union for the factory. Management is furious and immediately forbids workers from talking with the organizers. But when Norma's father drops dead from a heart attack in the factory, after being forced to work despite his chest pains, Norma gets interested in the union. The factory chiefs make her life a living hell and finally find a reason to fire her. As she waits for the police to come and get her, she scribbles "UNION" on a piece of cardboard and holds it wordlessly over her head. One by one, the factory workers shut down their machines in solidarity with Norma.

The union won. Martin Ritt's fine character study was about the rights of workers but also about the role of women in galvanizing large-scale change. Norma Rae discovers an inner strength she didn't know she had and feels she is, at last, doing something worthy.

Field immersed herself so entirely in the role of Norma. In a fearless performance, she was often drenched in sweat, a product of the intense Alabama heat, where looking fresh is nearly impossible. She did not care; it was all about truth for Field.

The cast was nicely rounded out, with Beau Bridges as Sonny and Leibman as the sharp New Yorker on a mission. But make no mistake, this film belonged heart and soul to Sally Field. Nominated for four Academy Awards, including Best Picture, the film won Oscars for Best Actress and the haunting song "It Goes Like It Goes."

An actress had been born at last.

“Field must have felt the earth move under her feet when the reviews for *Norma Rae* came out.”

“This version is stunning, a handsome, often beautiful production enhanced by superb music and the performances of Klaus Kinski and Isabelle Adjani.”

NOSFERATU THE VAMPYRE (1979)

DIRECTED BY Werner Herzog
COUNTRY Germany

The original *Nosferatu* (1922) offers a very different vampire. He looks like a living pestilence, something ugly and evil that will devour your soul. But it was likely the first film based on the famous gothic novel *Dracula*. Unfortunately, the producers failed to secure the rights to the book, so the film had to deviate from the original plot. The title cards also needed to change, so the Dracula in that early silent film became Count Orlock. This time, sixty years later, the makers did purchase the rights to the Stoker book, so the vampire could be called Dracula. Despite the challenges with copyright, the original movie was still an unsettling and frightening horror film, and most recognized the book despite the name changes.

When Herzog announced the remake, he made it clear he did not plan on making many changes. This version is stunning, a handsome, often beautiful production enhanced by superb music and the performances of Klaus Kinski and Isabelle Adjani as Lucy, the object of his affection.

Like the original *Nosferatu*, the vampire in this film is a monstrous-looking creature resembling a rat. Kinski portrays him with charisma and a sexual attraction that draws women to him. Very different from the suave, sophisticated men who have portrayed the part through the years (Bela Lugosi, Christopher Lee, Louis Jordan, Jack Palance, and Frank Langella), but this Dracula works. It has more in common with Gary Oldman's evolving and shape-shifting vampire in Bram Stoker's *Dracula* (1992), Francis Ford Coppola's operatic version of the tale.

Herzog fills the screen with frightening images, never going for the easy scare, allowing the terror to build with the Count's first appearance. The ship carrying Dracula and his coffins drifts aimlessly from the sea into the town's docks, empty save the vampire and dead Captain, who has lashed himself to the ship's wheel. The horde of rats aboard the ship then infests the town, as does the vampire by feasting on the townsfolk. The final scenes are unforgettable—the Count dead, betrayed by Lucy, who sacrifices herself to keep him up past sunrise, and that last image of Harker, now a vampire.

Opening in North America in 1979 during a horror extravaganza at the movies, the film was up against *Dracula* (1979), with Frank Langella recreating his Broadway role for the film. Laurence Olivier hampered that film with a dreadful performance, making his fierce vampire hunter look more like an elderly Jewish woman. After the final tally, *Nosferatu* fared much better.

Herzog utilizes the standards of great horror films, with night mists, fog, shadows, and a slow-building sense of dread throughout the film. Something terrible is coming—we know it, and so does Lucy.

Bringing sound to the narrative permitted Herzog to fill the screen with eerie noises and a bizarrely haunting musical score, adding immeasurably to this already frightening film. The 1979 version of *Nosferatu* is memorable and highly regarded even today, though the silent version is the more famous of the two.

Opposite Werner Herzog bravely remade the classic silent film, creating a breathtaking film with a vampire portrayed by Klaus Kinski, grotesque but strangely sexual. Haunting, it feels like a nightmare from which one cannot awake.

216

THE CHINA SYNDROME (1979)

DIRECTED BY James Bridges
COUNTRY USA

Opposite Art imitates life in this film about a nuclear accident released just as Three Mile Island happened in the United States. Jane Fonda earned her third consecutive Academy Award nomination.

The China Syndrome, the first American film to explore a nuclear accident within a power plant, was released on March 16, 1979. Incredibly, just twelve days later, there was a major nuclear accident at Three Mile Island in Pennsylvania. It was the first major incident within a nuclear power plant and dangerous enough to put it on high-security alert. Dangerously close to a "China syndrome," meaning the core melts into the earth, releasing deadly doses of radiation, the accident sent audiences flocking to cinemas to figure it all out.

Nuclear power is a clean and relatively inexpensive energy source, but we have seen in the last forty years just how fatal it can be. Chernobyl was a full-scale disaster, and the impact is felt to this day in and around the plant.

Three Mile Island could have easily been our Chernobyl, but thankfully never got that far.

James Bridges's electrifying thriller *The China Syndrome* explores the events surrounding a news crew who happened to be in the plant during a high-scale incident. Jack (Jack Lemmon) is the harried foreman who prevents an incident from escalating. Kimberly Wells (Jane Fonda) and her cameraman Richard (Michael Douglas) believe they have witnessed a near full-scale nuclear accident. They are forbidden to film it but do so anyway.

Kimberly investigates further, but the executives at the plant do not want it exposed because it will shut them down. Once they discover Jack cooperating with the reporters, we know his days are numbered. They eventually shoot him when he takes command of the plant by force. As he lies dying, he hears the machines whirring out of control. Once again, they are in the midst of a meltdown. Kimberly and Richard, with the help of Jack's friends and the damning information they have discovered, expose the plant as unsafe and on the verge of a China syndrome.

By 1979, Jane Fonda was on a career roll, and for *The China Syndrome*, she received her third consecutive nomination for an Academy Award as Best Actress. She beautifully captured the driven news woman striving to be taken seriously in a sea of men and who gets her chance with this tragic story. Jack Lemmon was a Best Actor nominee at the Oscars, a career renaissance beginning for him with three nominations over the next four years for Best Actor. As the distressed foreman, he was superb, terrified at what might be happening and haunted by his part in it. The third actor, Michael Douglas, gave a solid performance, furthering his growing movie career.

Bridges gave the film a startling urgency, as though he knew what was about to happen in Pennsylvania. It remains one of the most profound examples of life imitating art. And a frightening account of what could and eventually did happen with nuclear power.

“It remains one of the most profound examples of life imitating art.”

218 “Appearing brash, loud, and confident, she is nothing of the kind unless on stage; while off stage, she is vulnerable and terrified.”

THE ROSE (1979)

DIRECTED BY Mark Rydell
COUNTRY USA

Very few acting debuts have been as remarkable as that of Bette Midler in *The Rose*. Lady Gaga came close to rivalling her years later in *A Star Is Born* (2018). Midler was a well-known stage entertainer famous for her powerful voice and foul language, which she used liberally in her shows. Fearless, she was the perfect choice for this film, a thinly disguised biography of Janis Joplin. The script adopted much of Midler's persona for the film, and though portraying someone else, she is a variation of herself, which is no easy feat.

As Mary Rose Foster, Midler is a revelation, her character known as "The Rose." The intense pressures of being a rock star have impacted her terribly, and she turns to drugs and alcohol for respite. She has no filter and says whatever is on her mind, often landing herself in trouble. In concert, she is vulgar but an explosive performer the audiences adore. Offered the chance to meet her idol, a country singer named Billy Ray, portrayed by the great Harry Dean Stanton, she is humiliated when he demands she stop singing his songs. A profoundly decent man, he disapproves of her coarse language and behaviour on and off stage. Little does she know, her controlling manager Rudge (Alan Bates) arranged the meeting to win favour with him, wanting to sign the man to his label.

Humiliated and stunned, Rose escapes in a limo with a driver, Huston (Frederic Forrest), and the two set off on a cross-country road trip back to New York and fall in love. Seeing her at her worst, he loves her anyway and worries about her self-destructive path. Rudge realizes they can't be separated, even after telling disparaging stories about each of them to the other. He manages to convince her to perform again. Rose sings one song on stage in a drugged haze before collapsing and dying of an overdose.

Nicely directed by Mark Rydell, the film belongs to Midler, a whirlwind of energy, however destructive, throughout the film. Appearing brash, loud, and confident, she is nothing of the kind unless on stage; while off stage, she is vulnerable and terrified. She believes she has found true love with Huston and might be right.

Frederic Forrest is excellent as her lover Huston, one of two outstanding performances he gave in 1979, along with his role as Chef, the highly strung soldier in *Apocalypse Now* (1979) who loses his head to Kurtz (Brando).

Alan Bates is intensely dislikable as Rudge, her self-serving manager. Everyone around her knows he is a problem, but it doesn't hit Rose until much later.

Popular with audiences and critics, *The Rose* received four Academy Award nominations, including Best Actress (a given), Best Supporting Actor (Forrest), Best Film Editing, and Best Sound. Midler finished second in balloting for the prestigious New York Film Critics Award for Best Actress, behind Sally Field in *Norma Rae*, who swept the Best Actress awards.

Incredibly, the song "The Rose" was not nominated for an Academy Award, yet it has become one of the great love songs of the modern age.

Midler went on to do a great deal of film work but never reached these heights again. Years later, she received an Oscar nomination for her performance in *For the Boys* (1991), which she also produced. *The Rose* remains her career zenith.

Opposite Loosely based on rocker Janis Joplin, Bette Midler delivered a towering performance that she has never equalled.

220 THE TIN DRUM (1979)

DIRECTED BY Volker Schlöndorff
COUNTRY Germany

Opposite This controversial film was banned in several countries for its overt portrayal of sexuality, which would now be considered rather tame. Alarming and brilliant.

Banned in Ontario, Canada, to see the picture we had to go stateside to Buffalo or head over to Quebec, which a group of us did a year after it came out. We realized that the censors had cut out any suggestion of nudity, thereby losing much of the film, which accurately told the story from the acclaimed German novel by Günter Grass.

The Tin Drum was acclaimed around the globe, won the Cannes Film Festival Palm d'Or, tying with *Apocalypse Now* (1979) as Best Film, and later won the Academy Award as Best Foreign Language Film. Yet when I finally saw the whole film in 1980, it confounded me. Watching it again more recently, I found myself no more enlightened.

Are we watching an allegory about man's inhumanity to each other? Are we watching a film about the growing horrors as Nazism swept through Germany? Or are we merely watching a movie about an obnoxious, deeply disturbed little boy who decides to stop growing at the age of three? He is no Peter Pan, this Oskar (David Bennent), but an ever-watchful child who bangs relentlessly on his tin drum and, when angered or frightened, responds with an ear-piercing scream that breaks glass. That scream becomes Oskar's weapon against the world, his only defence for his tiny body.

While critics of the 70s hailed the film as an allegorical masterpiece, I found Oskar to be an ill-tempered, manipulative child who, when he fails to get what he wants, pounds that drum or unleashes his terrible scream. Granted, he is exposed to terrible horrors, but many of them are of his own doing. It becomes hard to feel anything for Oskar because he is such a cold, calculating little monster.

David Bennent, just eleven at the time, is extraordinary as Oskar, an outstanding performance. His burning eyes see what the world is and relay that message like an electric shock. Bear in mind, he stops growing outwardly but continues to age and is often driven by his lust. Part of the rationale for censoring was the scene with Oskar frolicking in bed with a nude woman. The censors' delicate sensibilities were offended, so several countries banned the film.

Directed by Volker Schlöndorff, who went on to guide Dustin Hoffman on stage and television as Willy Loman in *Death of a Salesman*, *The Tin Drum* contains many unforgettable images. But still, too many things left unanswered or unexplained in the film left some audiences befuddled. For years *The Tin Drum* was the most profitable German film to play in the United States and one of Germany's most successful films. To this day, it is revered as a work of art.

"It becomes hard to feel anything for Oskar because he is such a cold, calculating little monster."

ACKNOWLEDGMENTS

No one writes a book alone. So many joined me along the way, making my vision possible. Very much like a director making a film, surrounded by a cast and crew.

To begin, Robert Nichols and the Palazzo family, thank you so much for your belief in this project and me, and what lies beyond. You are tremendous, and have no doubt spoiled me. I hope there are many more projects with you. Rob, my friend, you altered the course of my life and brought to fruition a dream created long ago. I suspect we will be friends for life despite the ocean dividing us. I hope this book makes you proud.

To the great Karen Scanlan, my friend, my editor, how can I thank you? You made the book better with your gentle guidance, your wisdom, and literary intellect. This has reignited a long and beautiful friendship that started so long ago. I love you lady.

To my daughters, Aurora and Ariana, a constant inspiration, thank you. I love you both.

To Sherri, how I miss you, my girl. The sun is a little dimmer, the nights a lot lonelier, and I do not laugh as much. But you are with me, I know you are waiting for me, reading a good book under a tree, surrounded by your cats and dogs.

To my parents, who always have believed in my work, and saw beyond my many flaws to the artist within. Thanks Mom and Dad.

To Danny, Sharon, Gillian, Kevin F., Kevin McD, Ian and Dan E., my precious college crew, for your endless friendship, love, and support. Love you all very much.

Ellie Todd, as always. My grandfather Alex Foote, who taught me to do everything to the best of my ability.

My mentors, Jerry Smith, the late great Jim Peddie, George Hood, Susann Imshaug, Diane Lackie, the late John Crocker, David Toye, Rik Davie, and film friends, Peter Howell, Sam Weller, Mark Ingram, Rich Payne, Gemma Files, Scott Feinberg, and Clayton Davis.

My cousin and website partner, Alan Hurst and his partner Craig Leask, jumped into a long journey with me online and still believe in the thing.

I have always been guided by strong women in my life. Along with the amazing women I've already mentioned, I wish to thank my grandmother Anne Foote, who instilled in me a love for the written word, Joanne, Susan, Linda, Holly, Julie, Gemma, and all the other women I call mentors and friends.

And Nick Maylor, how I miss you my friend, my son. When I cannot sleep, I go online expecting to find you there, but no more. Life became too overwhelming for you, dear Nick. You were the greatest natural film writing talent known to me, unlike any I had seen before. Glad you touched my life even so fleetingly. A part of you is in this book.

PICTURE CREDITS

Every effort has been made to trace and acknowledge the copyright holders. If any unintentional omission has occurred, we would be pleased to add an appropriate acknowledgment in any future edition of the book.

t: top; b: bottom; c: centre; l: left; r: right

Courtesy of Alamy: 20 20th Century-Fox Film Corporation/ Everett Collection Inc; 24, 142, 156, 171, 175, 214, 221 Album; 12, 45, 74, 81, 127, 128, 167, 187, 193, 195 Allstar Picture Library Limited; 89 Colaimages; 111, 177 Collection Christophel; 82 Columbia Pictures/TCD/Prod.DB; 79 De Laurentiis/TCD/Prod. DB; 206 Entertainment Pictures; 16, 36, 64, 94, 120, 125 Everett Collection Inc; 139b Francis Specker; 115 Landmark Media; 69 LUCASFILM/COPPOLA CO/UNIVERSAL/Album; 201 Marka; 97 Masheter Movie Archive; 62, 116, 119, 122, 211 Moviestore Collection Ltd; Cover Paramount Pictures/Cinematic Collection; 19, 34, 76 Paramount/TCD/Prod.DB; 93, 101, 152, 172, 184, 199 Photo 12; 33, 99, 103 Pictorial Press Ltd; 6, 55, 105, 183, 196, 213 PictureLux/The Hollywood Archive; 23, 29, 30, 130, 133, 134, 159, 188 ScreenProd/Photononstop; 43, 47, 48, 61, 67, 70, 87, 90, 106, 108, 122, 137, 141, 145, 148, 151, 155, 161, 162, 164, 168, 179, 190, 202, 217, 218, 222 TCD/Prod.DB; 15, 57, 84, 139t, 146 United Archives GmbH; 39 Universal Pictures/TCD/ Prod.DB; 180 Universal/Everett Collection Inc; 26 WARNER BROS/Album; 73 WARNER BROS/Landmark Media; 40, 51, 52, 58 WARNER BROS/TCD/Prod.DB